# Praise

MW01101588

"A deeply interesting and impactful read."
~ Megan Epperson

"C. Rhalena's writing reaches out to your head and heart. With profound clarity, humor and overflowing love, she explains the importance of the emotions shared with each of us by the divine." ~ Lieutenant David Drain

"This week, life threw me for a loop. I've had a terrible time pulling myself together. So I curled up with a cup of tea to re-read *Choices for Joy*. It was exactly what I needed. Thank you C. Rhalena Renee, I again see there is good in this world and I am focusing on the joy that is life." ~ Brenda Metz

*Choices for Joy – Book 1 in* <u>*Vibrant Living Series*</u>

Cover Photograph by Lisa Langel

GilGaia Publishing

# Choices for Joy

## Activate Your Unlimited Potential of Joy

Photo by Lisa Langel

## C. Rhalena Renee, CSH

"Joy is yours when you sing your own song.
Joy is mine, I will always sing along with you.
Joy is ours when we sing together
and may it be so for the rest of our lives."

~ Shawna Carol

## Dedication

This book is dedicated to all the teachers in my life. To
those who have reflected my own shadows, I thank you
for bringing me the experiences, which brought the pain
and sorrow that has deepened my capacity for joy. To
those who showered me with love and support, I thank
you for sharing my joys as well as witnessing my sorrows.
You have been the wonder-filled field in which my life has
grown.

To Mother Gaia, our blessed planet, and all her children,
who have never failed to inspire and comfort me, I offer
my deepest gratitude. Your mountains, rivers, trees, two-
leggeds, creepy crawlers, winged ones and all my relations
have taught me more than any other teacher. I am
especially grateful to my allies: Buffalo, Spider, Kestrel,
Wolf and Hummingbird.

To the Angels, especially the Archangels Uriel, Raphael,
Gabriel and Michael, I offer great respect and an open
heart. Thank you for your patience with me when I failed
to understand that we have worked together from the
start. I appreciate your humor and personalities as much
as your invaluable assistance in my life and in the lives of
my clients and students.

I cannot possibly name all the people who have touched my life and brought me joy. I would like to mention just a few, who have been particularly pivotal in my life: Mellissae Lucia and Janis Lynne, my sister women who have stood by me through it all; Shawna Carol, Reverend Judith Laxer, Terri Rivera (Sings with Ravens), Pamela Gerke, Mr. Loland and Barb Frye, my teachers and mentors; Robert Wade and Michele Cacano Green – brother, sister and beloved compadres; Howard and Willow Jeane Lyman, who taught me to trust in community; and my family - especially Natalie and David Drain, who walk together in great love and joy and to Kailey Paige, who has always been a great joy in my life.

I give special thanks to Lisa Langel, my heart daughter, who has taught me so much about tenacity, love and commitment.

Finally, I want to thank the Ancestors whose spirit and wisdom have been an ever-present influence in my life. You are felt, remembered and loved.

Gratitude

I offer my deep gratitude to those who have helped me birth this book in its physical form. Thank you Jennifer Moultine and Megan Epperson for the editing and for your encouragement about my work. Thank you to Mellissae Lucia and Elizabeth Dobes for your input on design. Thank you Lisa Langel, Elizabeth Dobes and Suzy Wenger for the art that brought visual beauty to this project.

Hummingbird is a symbol of joy. Despite its small size it is capable of amazing feats. This totem brings the medicine of enjoying life, lifting the spirit and expressing love. You will see hummingbird throughout this book. May her medicine open your heart and heal your soul.

# Table of Contents

Photo by Lisa Langel

# More Joy Somewhere

I have always had joy in my life – in little bits or even in large chunks for short periods of time. When I was a teen I sought out places and times to myself so I could be in joy. I thought I should have more joy but didn't feel it was allowed. The seeking of quiet joy taught me the beauty of silence and of alone time.

I talk a lot about joy in my classes and to my clients. I share my joy in my music. Joy has called to me throughout my life and I have thought of myself as a relatively joyful person. However, I now understand how little expectation I had for living in joy.

This book started as a compulsion to call people to joy. I knew that just a little more joy in each person's life would shift our world into a healthier and more sustainable one. We would collectively be happier. In starting the book I received a delightful surprise. I was the first person called to live in more joy.

This is the first teaching: simply by opening to joy you attract more joy into your life. Whatever you place your focus on will become your teacher. In trying to share my knowledge and experience, joy and I became co-creative partners. And as we know, partners always have lots of things to teach us. As I began to write about joy, joy invited me into a deeper understanding and engagement.

I absolutely know that joy is the key to finding our soul purpose and life path. Joy will heal our lives and the planet. We are meant to be in joy; it is part of our essential makeup as humans. All of this I wanted to share. Then other things started getting in the way: my mother's surgery, my parents' struggle with moving in their 70s, my sister's coming into her empowerment, my other sister getting married, my friend going through a crisis. I could go on. I was surrounded by angst and change. It was intense, witnessing loved ones as they moved through significant transformations in their lives. Because I was writing about joy, I was acutely aware of how little it was being used to navigate these transformations.

I didn't understand this was part of the co-creative process with joy until something really challenging happened. My intestines decided to cramp, burn and generally give me a really hard time. Yes, I had been eating cheese, which tends to upset my digestion. But this was way beyond that. I didn't want to move. I was afraid to eat anything even when I felt hungry.

My dear friend, Mellissae Lucia, suggested I have a talk with my body and ask it what's going on. She specifically suggested the non-dominant hand technique. This is where you ask a question and then use your non-dominant hand to write the answer. The technique works pretty well to get to the core of things. It tends to bypass the logical, thinking brain that already has its ideas of what's going on.

So, I created sacred space and talked to my body. I began by singing/sounding "oo" tones to access the lower abdomen, where the pain was focused. When things began to shift I began asking questions. I'm going to share the conversation that followed. The *italicized* text is what came through the non-dominant writing as my body's wisdom.

What is this pain in my abdomen about?

*I'm cranky. I never get what I want!*

What do you want?

*Ease and comfort.*

What does that look like?

*I want to play, to run in the fields, to be surrounded by joyful ones. I want to be in joy. I'm tired of suppressing it.*

11

What will bring you joy today?

> *JOY ISN'T SOMETHING YOU BRING OR DO!*
> *Joy is something you follow. Stop talking about joy and follow it!!! It's everywhere. YOU KNOW IT. YOU KNOW IT!*
>
> *Take joy. Stop being joyfully small because of others. Just stop it. Expect more joy. Amplify it. Do it now!*

OK. I commit to following joy and to not limiting it because of others. I will be joy personified. I will be wholly myself.

After this conversation, I wept. It was true. I was holding joy at bay. A slide show of events moved across my mind showing how many times and in how many ways I was doing that. Some of these I'll share with you later in this book. It became crystal clear to me that I had only been dipping my toe into joy. I saw how many times I was criticized for being in joy, for being happy. I saw that it was not tolerated in the academic or corporate world. Even in my family and in other intimate relationships it was tolerated only in small amounts. I saw how often my relative joy drew people to me and then how they acted to extinguish the joy. And how often I let them succeed!

As soon as I committed to following joy, the pain and discomfort in my intestines eased. And the course and focus of my book changed. Joy and her teachings became co-writers.

A favorite spiritual song began running through my head.

> *There is more joy somewhere, there is more joy somewhere.*
> *I'm gonna keep on 'til I find it, there is more joy somewhere.*

I saw how even this delightful song actually put joy at a distance. I have changed the words and now sing:

> *There is more joy right here, there is more joy right here.*
> *I'm gonna keep on celebratin', there is more joy right here.*

Personal Reflection:

How much joy do you allow in your life? Can you identify ways in which you celebrate joy? Are there ways in which you limit joy or feel your joy limited by others?

When do you feel joy?

Where does joy feel centered in your body? Heart, belly, limbs, all over...?

# For Those Who Want
# To Know Why

Sometimes I absolutely need to know why. It's not that I doubt necessarily. It's more that I simply do not have enough knowledge or experience to judge what's being presented without more information. Or, I want to connect all the dots before I commit. If you share these feelings this section is just for you.

At other times, I have an immediate sense of the rightness of what's being presented. I don't need to know the why. I already intuitively trust it. In these cases I do not want to spend time with the whys. I want to just move on to the hows. If that's what you're feeling, please feel free to skip this section and go directly to the hows. You can always come back here later.

**Why is Joy Important?**

Studies on joy and happiness suggest we have lost a great deal of our ability to know what will bring us joy and happiness. We often anticipate great joy when we achieve something only to find a sense of let down when the achievement comes.

These studies are not surprising. We have become a culture of people who are told what we want, what's important and how we should live. This has been happening for centuries and, since the 1950s, with the increased availability to media sources, the barrage of messages telling us what we want has grown exponentially. In addition, life has become so fast and filled with so much stimulation that we do not easily have the time or the space in which to consider for ourselves what it is that we truly want.

Let's take an historical perspective and consider how quickly our lives changed in the last century. Henry Ford did not start making automobiles until 1908. And it would be decades before most Americans had one. The advent of the automobile introduced our ability to move quicker and farther with more flexibility. In post WWII, technology exploded in the household freeing the housewife from the long and tedious processes of washing clothes, cooking, baking, etc. Most of the daily chores were done by hand before WWII. The average home didn't have toasters, mixers or washing machines. In rural America, many folks still baked their own bread and made their own butter.

Today life is very different. For example we're no longer beating rugs out on the clothes line. Just plug in the vacuum. You can even do it wearing pearls like Mrs. Cleaver.

As most of us know, women's roles were quite limited before the 1940s. Women were primarily relegated to being mothers, nuns, and teachers. It wasn't until Florence Nightingale in the 1850s modernized nursing that being a nurse was considered a reputable profession. During WWII, women did work in factories and offices. When the men came back from the war, women were sent back home to be the wives, mothers and homemakers that their men had fought to preserve. Meanwhile, their work at home was diminished by technological advances. Women became displaced, and their lives became less significant. However, they knew what they were capable of after their success in the temperance movement and in women's suffrage as well as their experience stepping into traditional male roles during WWII. By the 1960s women were challenging gender roles and have since taken their place in corporate America, politics, healthcare and more.

Changes in gender roles, movement away from the extended family into the relative isolation of cities, and of course technology have all changed the texture of our lives.

We don't tend to have the same support systems. Most of us don't have an extended group of people witnessing our lives or noticing and encouraging our natural giftedness. We have lost the traditional rites of passage (like the first successful hunt for boys and the blue ribbon win for girls) that helped us define who we were. Yes, these may have been gender limiting, but they affirmed our ability to succeed and to provide for our family's needs. Local festivals and other traditions defined our community life. We knew the trees, lakes and parks in our area. They were part of our life and were sacred reminders of important moments.

Today, most of us live isolated lives where we do not even know our neighbor's names. We don't have time to get to know them. We are bombarded my messages that time is money, that money is necessary for happiness and that we have to get ahead and stay ahead.

Technology has not really given us the freedom we might have expected. Instead we are simply encouraged to do more because we can. The increased access to people's lives through technological mediums has created a barrage of noise constantly telling us what we should be and have. We are plugged into the world, but isolated from our family and neighbors – and most disastrously, from ourselves. We too seldom take the time to ask ourselves what it is we truly want or need in our lives.

Because of our isolation we are more likely to experience fear from the unknown around us. We don't have the comfort of familiarity with our immediate surroundings because we so rarely experience them directly. To illustrate this point, I'd like you to consider how many times you've heard on the news about a rapist, molester or murderer living in a neighborhood where no one suspected his/her presence. They show the neighborhood, and it could just as easily have been your neighborhood. You don't know your neighbors, and now your fear of being out in your own yard increases. The idea that the world is not safe is supported and you feel a certain level of threat. Because of this you are more likely to have negative thoughts and feelings about your neighbors as well as about life in general. However, these negative thought patterns actually decrease our ability to cope with our world. They interfere with our access to important personal resources. In contrast, positive emotions broaden our outlooks and help us to build resources.

Barbara Fredrickson, a positive psychology researcher at the University of North Carolina, published a landmark paper on the subject of positive thinking, which will give us some insight. (www.ncbi.nlm.nih.gov/pmc/articles/PMC3156028/)

She writes:

"Because positive emotions arise in response to

diffuse opportunities, rather than narrowly-focused threats, positive emotions momentarily broaden people's attention and thinking, enabling them to draw on higher-level connections and a wider-than-usual range of percepts or ideas. In turn, these broadened outlooks often help people to discover and build consequential personal resources. These resources can be *cognitive*, like the ability to mindfully attend to the present moment; *psychological*, like the ability to maintain a sense of mastery over environmental challenges; *social*, like the ability to give and receive emotional support; or *physical*, like the ability to ward off the common cold. People with these resources are more likely to effectively meet life's challenges and take advantage of its opportunities, becoming successful, healthy, and happy in the months and years to come. Thus, the personal resources accrued, often unintentionally, through frequent experiences of positive emotions are posited to be keys to later increases in well-being. Put simply, the broaden-and-build theory states that positive emotions widen people's outlooks in ways that, little by little, reshape who they are."

People with these resources are most likely to create or co-create ways to heal our world.

In his article in the Huntington Post - *The Science of Positive Thinking: How Positive Thoughts Build Your Skills, Boost Your Health, and Improve Your Work -*

James Clear discussed Fredrickson's work. His closing comments included this directive:

"To put it simply:
Seek joy, play often, and pursue adventure.
Your brain will do the rest."

## Foreboding Joy

Dr. Brené Brown is well known for her work on vulnerability and joy. In doing research for one of her many books, Dr. Brown found something she was not looking for and did not expect. In 12 years of research, she discovered not one person described themselves as joyful who did not also have a practice of gratitude. By practice, she means a specific and ongoing activity in which gratitude is acknowledged. Such practices include: keeping a gratitude journal; sharing gratitude for the day around the dinner table; and beginning and/or ending each day with gratitude. Dr. Brown concluded that practicing gratitude invites joy into our lives.

Like most people, Dr. Brown was raised to believe that vulnerability is weakness. She now knows and teaches us that vulnerability is the courage to be daring, to ask for what you need. You can't have true courage without opening up to your vulnerability.

As Dr. Brown says, "Vulnerability is not about winning, it's not about losing. It is about having the courage to show up and be seen."

Dr. Brown explains that joy is by far the most terrifying emotion we will ever face. It's because we have lost our tolerance for vulnerability. As a result, joy becomes foreboding.

Listening to her, I realized how common *foreboding joy* is in our world. It happens when we notice how well things are going – great job, good relationship, beautiful children – and then we imagine something happening to ruin it. My mother would often say in those situations, "I wonder when the other shoe will drop?" The other shoe was hardship, sorrow or pain. I remember literally looking over my shoulder for that other shoe. I could feel it hovering. The moment of joy we feel at our good fortune can makes us feel vulnerable because we can immediately sense the pain of losing it. So we diminish the joy immediately by imagining the worst happening. We forebode the joy.

Dr. Brown suggests we can move away from foreboding joy by moving into gratitude. As we look at our beautiful children sleeping peacefully, we speak our gratitude for them in our lives. As we gaze into the eyes of our beloved, we tell them specifically why we are grateful for them. We speak of the ideal job we have with gratitude. We do all these things as a practice. This allows joy to take hold and stay with us.

Dr. Brown has authored many books including *Daring Greatly*. You can also listen to her on YouTube.

## Molecules of Emotion

Joy is just one emotion. The Angels tells us that joy cannot be fully experienced if we suppress other emotions (see page 63). In her groundbreaking work, Dr. Candace Pert tells us the science behind this assertion.

Dr. Pert's research provides scientific evidence that a biochemical basis for awareness and consciousness does exist. The mind and body are indeed one. Our emotions and feelings are the bridge that links the two.

Dr. Pert identified what she calls the opiate receptor as part of her doctoral research. Receptors sit on the surface of cells. We have hundreds of thousands of receptors on the average cell and specialized cells such as neurons might have millions of receptors surrounding them. These receptors act as tiny sensors, which wait until the exact chemical key comes along that will fit into them. They're like a security key that is made to only fit into one specific lock. These chemical keys are called ligands. The most common ligand (accounting for nearly 95% of all ligands) is known as a (neuro)peptide. The peptide delivers its chemical message to the receptor on the cell, which then transmits its message deep within the cell. This triggers a chain of biochemical reactions, which can create huge changes within the cell. These changes can be of a positive or negative nature in terms of health and well-being. The receptors and the peptides make up the molecules of emotion.

Dr. Pert's research shows us that when emotions are expressed all systems in our body become united and are made whole. When emotions are repressed, when we deny them, when we do not allow them to be whatever they may be, our network pathways get blocked. The flow of the vital feel-good unifying chemicals that run both our biology and our behavior simply stop.

Dr. Pert says, "I believe all emotions are healthy, because emotions are what unite the mind and the body. Anger, fear, sadness, the so-called negative emotions, are as healthy as peace, courage and joy. To repress these emotions and not let them flow freely is to set up a dis-integrity in the system, causing it to act at cross-purposes rather than as a unified whole. The stress this creates, which takes the form of blockages and insufficient flow of peptide signals to maintain function at the cellular level, is what sets up the weakened conditions that can lead to disease. All honest emotions are positive emotions. Health is not just a matter of thinking 'happy thoughts.' Sometimes the biggest impetus to healing can come from jump-starting the immune system with a burst of long-repressed anger."

Dr. Pert discovered that neuropeptides and their receptors are the substance of our emotions and that they are in continual communication with our immune systems. The immune system is the mechanism through which health and disease are created. Stress-related diseases can be seen as an information overload; the mind-body network is so taxed by unprocessed sensory input in the form of suppressed trauma or undigested emotions it has become bogged down and cannot flow freely.

Eastern healers, indigenous practitioners and alternative therapists may not have ever seen a peptide or measured a receptor, but they have known the truth of this connection between our emotions and our health.

Many of us recognize the power of our emotions on an intuitive level. When we're happy, we feel better. When we finally tell someone they have made us angry, we feel better. When we are wholly present in our own lives - embracing our full spectrum of emotional capacity (and expressing those emotions appropriately) – we feel better.

This book is specifically about making choices to live in joy. The above research clarifies that joy and all the other emotions are a package deal. If you want joy, you must be willing to dance with the other emotions. In my experience, when you do, you find joy in the other emotions. The stories throughout this book will help illustrate this concept.

Personal Reflection

What is your emotional repertoire? Take a moment
and jot down all the emotions that you have felt in
your life. Notice how familiar you are with each
emotion. Let yourself notice any judgments you have
about each specific emotion.

Are you aware of any emotions that you have never
experienced or don't let yourself feel?

Are you aware of any time in which you forbade joy
(times when you let fears or thoughts of potential
hardship interfere with joy in the moment)?

If so, take a moment and return to the joy. Let
yourself feel it. Speak your gratitude for the situation.
Let the joy return.

Notes:

# Here and Now:
## The Dance with Joy

We have become a culture that tends to look to the future when things will be better – when we have more money, more love, a bigger house, the promotion, etc. Our desires can seem always just out of reach. This is bad form, stressful and incredibly dis-empowering. Hopefully we wake up and realize we're wasting our time in the pursuit while totally missing the joys in the present moment. Too often we come to this when we're old and alone. Let's take a more proactive and positive approach.

Wise ones and spiritual teachers tell us that whatever we need or want, we have within ourselves. That's right. We already have it. If we focus there, we can spend our time in the present, the now, right here. And we can enJOY it now, instead of waiting. Here's how it works:

Let's say I want to open a bookstore and cafe. Further let's say that I have no experience in retail or business or restaurants. But I really want to open a bookstore and cafe. How can I tell you that I already have that within me? Here's the test:

Can I dream it in detail?

Yes! *I can smell the books and imagine walking through the shelves and touching them. I see how cozy it is, with comfortable chairs scattered here and there. From the other side of the store, I can smell coffee and spiced teas and homemade muffins. I see the sandwich board with sandwich and salad offerings for the day. And I see regular customers asking for "my usual". I see new folks peeking in the window, seeing something that sparks their interest and walking in to put their hands on a book or to inhale deeply the scent of their favorite bakery item. I see myself opening boxes of books and lovingly putting them on the shelves. I see me arranging author events and storytelling hours. I hear the click of the lock on the door as I close for the evening and I feel the satisfaction of heart-centered work and I sigh contentedly.*

I am absolutely delighted and in incredible joy as I visualize this. So yes, it is within me. Does that mean it will sprout in front of me and all I have to do is walk into it? Of course not. This is something I get to build. And to begin enjoying my bookstore cafe, I start with developing the skills and experience I need to manifest it. Here's where folks can lose track of the joy.

Lots of people will put their beautifully visualized dream off to the side or pin it on a board or in some other way put it outside of themselves. They say, "that is the goal, out there, someday, somewhere." They've just made their dream less possible and definitely less exciting and joyful. No, it's not their fault. We're usually taught to do just that.

It's great to have visual representations for our dreams through vision boards or other means. I'm not saying not to do that. I'm cautioning you not to leave the dream there - outside of you and your present life. Let the visual inspire you and to reflect the dream you carry inside of you.

When we are excited about something we want to share it with people in our lives. It can be helpful to speak your dreams. However if we don't choose our listeners wisely we often get comments like this:

> *You can't open a bookstore when you have no retail experience.*
> *A cafe? You can't even make a decent cup of tea.*
> *You'll never get the money for something like that in this economy.*

Let's admit it, we've all received comments like this from well meaning friends and family. And we've said this type of thing to a loved one ourselves. Why? Perhaps we think the person is really wasting their time or is being highly impractical. Sometimes we fear the person's success will take them away from us. Often we just don't want to see them hurt, so we squash the dream before it has time to take root. Let's stop the dream squashing, now.

Even if we can resist the dream squashers, too often our dreams suddenly become something that will take a lot of hard work and lots of sacrifice. So, we set ourselves up for deprivation and put our nose to the grindstone. What an expression! It even sounds painful. The first thing that gets ground off of our proverbial nose and our intuitive knowing is the joy!

We *can* do it differently. We can begin fulfilling our dream and experiencing its joy from the very beginning. Here's what that looks like.

*I have a dream of opening a bookstore cafe. Today, I am beginning that manifestation. Today I am making a list of what is needed to be successful. At the very top of the list is:*

> *Have a detailed dream (visualize, feel it manifest)*
> *Believe in the dream*
> *Be willing to do what is takes to manifest the dream*
> *Live the dream starting now*
> *Make a list of what is needed to realize the dream,*

.....

Notice that all of these things are stated in the present tense and the first four can be checked off immediately. You have begun the manifestation. You are in fact living the dream. You are unfolding it now.

With each step you take, STAY in the present. For example:

- Instead of saying, "I'm taking business courses so eventually I can open a bookstore cafe," frame it like this: "I am taking business courses. That's what successful bookstore cafe owners do. And I am a burgeoning successful bookstore cafe owner." Own the dream and experience the joy.

- Don't think, "I'm waiting tables until I can eventually open my own place. Think, "I am waiting on tables in a cafe and learning more about what it means to be the successful bookstore cafe owner I know that I am."

You get the gist. Try on as many aspects of your dream as you are able. Oh, and enJOY it!

The key is to actively hold the dream in every step of achieving it. And do so with the expectation that even if it is challenging, even if the task is not exactly your favorite aspect, you enJOY the fact that you are revealing more and more of the successful bookstore cafe owner that is within you. Every step is another unveiling.

In this scenario, there is no putting off joy and happiness. You are in the dream, it is happening, and you can literally check off items on your list that prove to you it is so. These items on your list become markers of your success. Celebrate each marker. I'm not suggesting a big party every time you pass a test or put another $20 in your savings for the down payment. Life can be celebrated in small ways. As you deposit that $20, take a moment and allow yourself to feel your dream being more realized. Maybe you smile and look in the mirror and say, "Good Job! I know you can do it. Every dollar is one step closer to standing in your own bookstore cafe. That $20 will purchase a couple books or flour for 100 muffins!" Find what works for you and don't allow these steps to become just another task. Celebrate the joy.

Here's another secret. When you dream your dream of the bookstore cafe, be certain to dream your entire life. *I own my dream business. I enjoy sharing it with my friends. It supports my loving family, who come in everyday. Being my own boss let's me travel and take an hour off in the morning to walk my dog. I am a respected member of my community and participate in little league or the Downtown association…*

While you are gathering the tools and experience necessary to reveal the successful bookstore cafe owner, you must also attend to these other details. Enjoy your friends at every step along the way – otherwise you may not have friends to share the dream with. Take time with family. Meet people and be open to enduring relationships. Get a dog, or walk someone else's dog from time to time. The point is to live the whole life you want to live right now. It might be a smaller version, but that's OK. The point is to enJOY your life here and now instead of waiting until it's picture perfect.

When my niece, Kailey, was about 5 years old she taught me a very important lesson. We were out doing errands and some grocery shopping. She loves sprinkle doughnuts, so we got a couple. When we got home we sat down to eat the doughnuts.

Kailey turned to me. "Auntie?"

"Yes," I said.

She paused for several seconds until she knew that she had my undivided attention and knew that I knew she was about to say something very important.

"There's no such thing as too many sprinkles," she stated. Then she turned back to her doughnut and ate.

At the time I was working 3 jobs to get my career going. I had very little time for play. She could see that I was limiting the "sprinkles" in my life and was asking me to stop. She may have saved my life with her gentle wisdom.

I pass her wisdom on to you and encourage you to notice and partake of the unlimited supply of "sprinkles" in your life.

## Personal Reflection

Take a moment now and consider what dream you are working toward – or perhaps what dream you have that needs to be recovered.

Sit with your dream – imagine what it feels like to live it, feel it, smell it, see it, touch it, taste it! Allow yourself to dive into a sensual experience of living the dream. Don't limit yourself – dream big and deep!

If you have found that dream, you can live that dream. What do you now have that brings you closer to the full realization of that dream? Remember, if you can truly see yourself in the dream - that counts. Celebrate that. Be grateful for the ability to dream it for that is the first and perhaps most powerful step in living it.

Now pick 2 or 3 things you will need to do to move closer to realizing the dream. How are you living those now? Remember, even if it's something like going to school next quarter, you can begin it now by applying to (or even Google-ing) the school to get the information about what people who do what you dream do. Everything you do gets you further into the dream. Celebrate it.

Notes:

# Dreams and Joy

Here's more motivation. If you live in the dream from the start you will notice when the dream shifts. Yep, our dreams change and shift. A dream launches us onto a particular path, but it does not always end up being the ultimate dream. Sometimes it is a stepping stone, a very vital stepping stone. Sometimes we have to walk part of a path to find the road that leads to our true path. A dream takes us on a path into the forest of our life, where we encounter many other paths. It is easy to get lost in this forest if we don't have a compass.

Joy is the compass we have been given to navigate our way into and through the forest. This is why we must actively keep our dreams - and the joy they bring - with us. If we have no expectation of joy until we ultimately realize the dream, we are likely to get lost in the forest. When we follow joy, we notice whether or not the path we're on has it. If we cannot

find joy where we are or if the joy of the path is no longer present, it is time to take a new path.
To illustrate, let me share some paths in my life's forest.

As a child, I always wavered between wanting to be a doctor or a nun. I really wanted to be both, but thought I couldn't be. As I got older, the idea of being a nun was less appealing, so I followed the sciences with the idea of becoming a doctor. The sciences came easy to me, and I ended up tutoring calculus, algebra, kinesiology and anatomy. But at some point, they became boring because they were not challenging enough. I was good at them, but they gave me little joy. At that time I was taking a class called Images of Western Man. In this class, three different professors presented what was happening in their discipline during a particular time frame in Western history. It fascinated me. I loved the big picture as well as the interweaving of cultural events, scientific breakthroughs and literature.

This led me to studying anthropology, which I eventually did graduate work in. And the work I was drawn to in anthropology was cross cultural spiritual traditions and resource management (to heal the planet). This was a very intellectually stimulating path, but I eventually figured out that most of the jobs were desk jobs, which I could never see myself doing. I was pretty angry that I spent all that time in school and I felt a bit lost. I sold real estate for money while I figured out what was next. It was new and interesting.

In real estate, I discovered that many of the skills I learned in resource management were transferable. It was good to know I hadn't wasted all those years. I enjoyed working with people to help them find a home that truly suited them. After a while, however, I noticed real estate agents seemed to be working all the time and that wasn't very healthy for me. I knew I had to leave it. I was offered a job with the Realtors® Association. It wasn't my dream job, but it did give me time to do more spiritual things, which led me to volunteering and eventually to a job as a youth minister. I discovered a deep love for working directly with people, and my anthropology background gave me very unique insight and understanding. The path of youth minister held lots of joys for me, but ultimately I burned out because of the church politics.

I was lost again in the forest for about a year. I found blips of joy, but nothing sustainable. It was clear I had lost my way. I found work. I liked the people I worked with. I was exploring my spirituality. I wasn't exactly unhappy, but my life was missing something. I felt there was something more I could be doing.

I started carrying the question, "what could I do to be of best use in the world?" During this time, I experienced a lot of trauma and loss. Several relationships ended. I had a falling out with my family. Loved ones died. I left my church.

Looking back, I understand that this was a time of undoing or becoming undone. This will happen at least once in a lifetime. I lost so much that I became open to new things and to new ways of walking in the world. I found myself drawn into new experiences and to people who were different in my life. I started seeing ads for a massage school. Massage was something I had never even been aware of before, yet it pulled me. It felt right, I went to massage school. Massage opened an entirely new world to me. Working with the physical body led me into working with the energetic body, the emotional, mental and spiritual bodies and eventually into being a spiritual healer and teacher.

I did not know what a spiritual healer was as a child. I had no reference except doctor and nun. I really wanted to be both. And the strength of that desire never truly left me. Being a spiritual healer is the biggest source of joy in my life. I can feel it pulsing beneath my breastbone. Before I knew what it was, I could sense the joy it would bring. Looking back, I can connect the dots and see how my initial desire (to be a doctor and a nun) played out in a world with no direct path to it. When I consider all the crossroads and how I made decisions at them, I am aware of two things. First, I had a sense of following something that I can best describe as an invisible chord that tugged me in various directions. I understand that chord to be the initial intention I set out. Second, I am aware that feelings of discontentment often arose to let me know I was off my path. At least, I was clear when a path no longer held any joy for me, and I was able to turn from it.

The point is we cannot see the future or where our path will take us. We can send our desires and intentions out into the world through commitment to a goal, but we also need to hold it loosely. It is a balance between trusting in our own knowing of what we desire and trusting that the universe will provide, but possibly in ways we cannot imagine.

My knowing that I wanted to serve as a healer and in a spiritual capacity was very strong and I unconsciously kept choosing paths that eventually took me to spiritual healing. I believe as small children we actually do know what it is that we are to do in this lifetime. Like me, we don't always have a context for what we want to do. But we always have a drive toward it. We tend to be attracted to things that are similar or that use the same skills. These may spark a dream and by all means we should follow it. We should also allow ourselves the freedom to leave the path if we no longer feel joy in it. Other paths will always open before us. Follow the joy. Keep it and the dream close.

When we hold a dream out away from us and put it on a "someday, somewhere" shelf with the mindset that we're going to have to work hard and do a lot of things we don't like in order to eventually get there, we lose track of our joy. We don't expect joy in the process. We focus on the tasks and steps along the way with a sort of tunnel vision. When we complete that last task and finally look around for the expected joy it's too often not there. And, let's face it, that's a pretty big let down.

One of my favorite clients was very good at stating a goal and defining the steps needed to get to the goal. She became overly reliant on focusing on the steps rather than her goal. Too often in a session she would want to work with why she wasn't able to achieve a particular step. As we talked about what was happening in her life, it would become clear to me that a new path had opened to her achieving her ultimate goal, and she couldn't see it because she was focusing on achieving one of her defined steps to that goal. This caused her a great deal of pain and frustration.

As Carlos Castaneda's Don Juan says, "there are many pathways into and out of the forest." By bringing her awareness back to her original goal, my client was able to see pathways that were presenting themselves. When she initially dreamed achieving her goal, she could not have imagined some of the paths that were now presenting themselves. She eventually learned to relax and open to pathways beyond her imagination while she takes steps to the center of her forest.

It's great to have goals and to discern the steps to those goals. However, we must remember that along the way life happens, Spirit moves and our dreams sometimes morph into something more powerful and joy-filled than we can imagine. By staying present with the dream we are more able to notice these shifts and changes. And, of course, we remember to *live* the dream and enJOY it!

It is time for us to allow more ease into our lives. It is time to actually question whether we're on the right track when our road becomes hard. Too often we assume it's only hard because that's part of the sacrifice of getting what we want. Sometimes, it's hard because it's an unworthy use of our resources.

Personal Reflection

How are you doing? Do you have joy on the path you are currently walking? If not, is it because you are not allowing yourself to experience the joy – or, because the path holds no joy for you?

Is everything about it hard?

Even in the challenging places, do you find satisfaction, joy, ease,…?

Do you remember why you are doing what you're doing? Can you see the goal? Are you able to feel what it will be like to have fully achieved it? What is that feeling?

Is the goal truly yours – or something you're holding/doing for someone else? It can be both, it's important that it is yours.

# Understanding
## Sacrifices for Joy

"No pain, no gain" could be the mantra of the Western world, particularly America in the last half century or more. We have come to believe that life is hard, full of pain and sacrifice. I'd like to talk about sacrifice and return us to a more balanced, useful and true definition of it.

Historically, women have been trained to put themselves last and to give everything for their families. Men have been trained to prioritize the job and support the family financially – above all else. This gender specific enculturation has morphed certainly and we are no longer so defined by gender. But interestingly we haven't necessarily learned to share these tasks. Instead, we've learned to add the burdens of the other gender's enculturation to our own. I am reminded of the Enjoli perfume add in the late 70s with the woman singing, "I can bring home the bacon, fry it up in a pan, and never never let you forget you're a man." The feminist movement birthed the "superwoman" who could do it all, and they in turn created a "superman" who also tries to do it all. Everybody thinks they can do more and should have more. But the cost is very dear indeed.

Technology can make our lives easier; it has many advantages. However, it has increased the pace of our lives to unhealthy extremes and we've come to believe technology can do just about anything better than we can do ourselves. In many ways we've come to rely on it to raise our children. The TV, the xbox and the wii have too often become nannies for our children. A significant number of our children are growing up into adults with challenged social and empathetic skills. They have not been mentored by consistent and loving attention from adults. We have learned to replace real intimate human connection with virtual realities found in video games, TV, Facebook, etc. Many believe that 500 Facebook friends equals an active fulfilling life.

And of course, we could talk about how our fast paced sterile world has affected our health as we consume quick, processed foods that have no nutritional value and have depleted our resources. But they give us the time we believe we need to get and do more and more and more. At least until we're sick and out of the game completely. This is the "sacrifice" of modern life.

Don't worry, we *can* change things. But before we can do anything of significance, I believe we need to understand sacrifice. It has come to mean for us giving up something because we *have to* in order to do/be/get what we're suppose to do/be/have. We praise those who give up the most. However, we fail to truly look at how what we gave up has affected our lives and the world.

We have failed to ask how our sacrifice has made anything or anyone more sacred. *Sacred* is the root of the word. A sacrifice should indeed make everything and everyone involved more sacred.

How often have we forced ourselves to do something we don't want to do so someone else can have something we have judged that they want or need? How often have we then complained or felt hurt because our "sacrifice" was not appreciated?

A true sacrifice is done willingly, with joy and with a knowing that the outcome is not in our hands.

I offer this as a guideline. If you are considering giving up something (making a sacrifice) ask yourself if you are truly willing to do it or if you are feeling forced into it. Can you offer the sacrifice with joy? These are two things only you can know and answer.

One mother can joyfully work two jobs to save money to send her child to college because that child dreams of being a doctor. This mother can carry the joy of knowing she is serving her child through the long hours of work and can radiate that joy to the child, which in turn motivates the child to do what he can do himself to realize their now shared dream.

Another mother can work two jobs for the same reason, but resent it because her own personal dreams are being lost in the process. But she feels "forced" into doing it because she wants to be a "good mother". Her child feels the resentment, sees that giving up one's dreams is expected and so forces herself to adhere to that expectation and goes to college instead of following her dream to be an auto mechanic.

Being a spiritual healer and listening to people's stories for almost two decades I can tell you that this happens a lot. I have had women crying as they tell me they gave up everything for their children, and now they don't even see them except at Christmas. I've had young men share how hard they've tried to live up to the expectations of their fathers when their hearts have always wanted to follow another path. I have heard husbands talk about how their wives worked so hard and stressed themselves – and everyone in the house – to make the perfect birthday celebration for him when all he wanted was a nice quiet evening at home with his wife. I've sat with the couple who comes to see me because the husband is always working and spends little time with his wife because he wants to save the money so some day he can take her on a world cruise.

In the last couple years, my most common client is the mother with small children who feels like a failure because she cannot keep up with the expectations to do and be everything. She has no time for herself. She worries that she's not meeting the needs of her children. She feels like she has nothing for herself. Without fail, this mother tells me that everyone else – all the other mothers – seem to be able to keep it all together. One week, I had three different mothers tell me this story, and I knew all three were friends. I asked them all if they'd shared their feelings with others. They were all afraid to let the others know they were struggling.

It's time for us to stop. It's time for us to consider other options. It's time for us to talk to each other about our dreams and desires. It's time for us to follow joy. It will never lead us astray.

Consider the woman who gave up her dreams to work two jobs for her child's college fund. What if instead she had followed her dream, followed the joy of it and opened herself in this way to the abundance of the Universe? What if in doing so she showed her child how to do the same? What if that child followed her joy and allowed the Universe to flow abundance into her life?

We cannot see with any certainty the future. What we can see most clearly is the present. From that viewpoint - and with some effort to speak with those in our lives about what's important to us – we can find and follow our joy. Sometimes that will bring us an opportunity to offer something in sacrifice – offer something that will indeed make everything and everyone involved more sacred. The only way we can judge that now, in this moment, is if we can willingly and joyfully make the offering without any attachment to the outcome. If you cannot do this, then I suggest the offering is not worthy of you or of others.

This not being attached to the outcome is a bit tricky, isn't it? Usually some desired outcome is what inspires a potential sacrifice. I want to go to the hottest rock concert of the year, so I will get a job and sacrifice my freedom. I want my children to have everything they need to be successful in their lives, so I will work two jobs to give them everything. I want my wife to be happy, so I'll work overtime, so we can go on that cruise and spend time together.

Yes, this is a tricky slope! Is a 3-hour concert worth weeks of less freedom? Maybe it is and maybe this sacrifice teaches us that working can give us a different kind of freedom. If we can do that willingly and joyfully, it is a worthy sacrifice.

Is working two jobs actually going to give your children everything they need? What if what they really need is to have you present and active in their lives? What if the most valuable thing you have to offer them is your laugh, your comforting arms when they fall, your witnessing of their everyday life? I encourage you not to assume young ones do not know what's good for them. Yes, it's your job to anticipate some of their future needs and to prepare for that. But they also have valuable and credible input about what they need. Asking them what they need helps them find and use their voice, trusting that they will be heard.

How many times have we given up something, so we can have the something we gave up? For example, how much sense does it make to give up time with your wife to work overtime, so you can have time with your wife on a romantic cruise? Yes, it sounds obviously flawed, but we've all probably done something similar. Our intention may be to offer something special, like the cruise. But sometimes we forget to ask if the others who are involved are willing to share the consequences of our sacrifices.

I remember a *Love Boat* episode with a couple in their 60s who finally got enough money to take their dream cruise. During the cruise the wife surprised her husband with a huge financial portfolio. They were rich! She had spent their entire married life skimping - using the same tea bag three times – to save money for their retirement. She had been investing every little penny she saved and had accumulated a million dollars in investments. The husband was shocked and then angry they had lived so frugally and he had worked so hard when they could have enjoyed their lives more all along the way instead of waiting to do it in retirement. Of course, he forgave her and might have even adjusted to his new financial standing. The point is she made a "sacrifice" that involved both of them without his knowing and therefore without his willingness. He despised the penny pinching and never told her. It is not right to carry people in our lives in this way. It robs us of joy.

Remember that "sacrifice" has been misused in our culture. It has even perhaps been a way to control us. In little ways, we can see this. If you want the girl (or boy) you have to look, smell and act a particular way, and we sell the products that will get you there. Just $9.99. If you want your children to succeed, they must have and do everything. Wait, there's more…..

We spend our time making money to afford the products and services that will get us what we're suppose to want. We're told "no pain, no gain." Or we are promised that in the end, even in the afterlife, we will get our just reward. And they are absolutely right. If we indeed give up things with no grace, no willingness, no joy – we will always be unhappy and unfulfilled: that is the recipe we are following. If we joyfully, willingly and with consciousness make an offering that will make everything involved more sacred our lives will be sacred *now*. Follow the joy and you will be in right relationship.

Personal Reflection

What sacrifices have you made in the past to reach a goal? Have you done them willingly and with awareness?

*It's never too late to go back, acknowledge the sacrifice and be willing to have offered it. We can look back and see perhaps that we were a bit stingy with the sacrifice through resentment, attitude or smallness. Those are all contractions that you may still be holding onto. Go back in your mind's eye. Do what you did but this time release your resistance and offer it freely.*

In what ways have your sacrifices made you and everyone else involved more sacred? Are you/they more highly valued or more deserving of respect? Have your sacrifices – in either a small or large way – connected you to spirit?

Notes:

# **W**hat Does It Mean to Follow Joy?

I have been talking a lot about following joy. But what does that really mean? How do I find it, so that I can follow it?

What is joy?

Webster defines joy as "the emotion evoked by well-being, success, or good fortune or by the prospect of possessing what one desires."

Synonyms for joy are blessedness, bliss, blissfulness, felicity, gladness, happiness, warm fuzzies.

We've all felt these in our lives. Joy is not an unknown. We experience it watching a movie, touching a loved one, sharing our special moments, swinging on a swing, drinking a cold beer after a hard day's work.

Joy has many faces. It shows up around us without any effort on our part.

We've been taught however not to trust joy. Like happiness it is fleeting. And perhaps it is. But fleeting suggests movement. It's here and then it moves on. We can be disappointed that it is no longer with us or we can follow it. Yes, that's right, follow it!

Too often we feel joy in a moment, and we want to freeze it. We want nothing to change. We grasp it and try to recreate the exact texture and detail of the moment. This is almost impossible to do. Consider this: the moment itself changed you. Joy touched and transformed you. If it didn't, you would not have noticed it. Even you are different. How can the joy the old you experienced be duplicated?

The joy cannot be grasped and we experience it as fleeting. However, we can open ourselves to experiencing more moments *like* it. We can take the joy in, allow ourselves to fully experience it and add gratitude to expand the joy. In this way we can become a beacon for joy, drawing it safely to our harbor.

Like attracts like. If we allow ourselves to be in the joy that we experience we will draw more joy to us. The new joy might look different, but it will be joy. If we choose to radiate the joy we experience instead of hiding it away like some endangered treasure, we draw more joy to us.

Beware of mistaking the joy for the circumstances that created it. Take a look at this example. Jenny's boyfriend surprised her one day at work by bringing her flowers. The gesture was so unexpected that joy bubbled up and wrapped her in a very big "warm fuzzy". He had never done anything like that before. The boyfriend was so pleased with her response that a few weeks later he once again brought her flowers. Because it was now not so unusual, Jenny did not experience the same level of joy. Her disappointment in not having the same level of feeling led her to become critical of her relationship. Was she losing interest, she wondered? Her cooler response made him question the same thing.

It is easy to equate the details with the joy. *Boyfriend brings flowers equals I am overwhelmed with joy. I should expect that same joy every time he brings me flowers. If I don't, something is wrong.* Don't go there. The first event changed both of you in terms of expectations. Joy can still be experienced, but you must let it be what it is. The first time was a joyful surprise. The second time may be a joyful acknowledgment of the sweetness of the first joy. They're not the same, but they're both joy. Take it. Build on it. Soak in it. Let it be what it is.

Personal Reflection

Reflect on a situation where joy was present for you. How did you engage with it? Did you diminish it or follow it?

Commit this week (or even just this day) to noticing where joy shows up in your life and allow yourself to follow it. Note the experience and where you feel it in your body. How does it affect the rest of your day or week?

# Angels on Joy

I long suspected that joy was more important than we realized. When the Angels came in 2006 and asked me to work with them, they became great teachers on the subject of joy.

Joy is a gift of great proportion. It eases us, brings comfort, makes us giggle, laugh, smile. It makes us feel delight and gives us the warm fuzzies. Anything can potentially bring us joy. Even hardship can carry joy when we know it's for a worthy cause.

Yes, the Angels have taught me a great deal about joy. I sat for a while trying to accumulate from my memory everything they have taught me through group Angel Readings, conversations and through my work with clients. Eventually, I realized it would be more efficient to just connect with the Angels and ask them to speak about joy. Here's what they offer:

Channeled info from the Angels on Joy:

> *"It pains us to see how little joy humans take in.*
> *Joy is everywhere, and it is freely available. Yet,*
> *you have learned to distrust it. You still can't resist*
> *it, but you take such little sips of joy.*
>
> *And so, your capacity for joy dwindles. And with*
> *it, your capacity for all other emotions dwindles.*
> *You must understand that all of the emotions are*
> *tied together. When you inhibit one, you inhibit*
> *them all. Your capacity to feel diminishes, and your*
> *spirits waver. This imbalance creates all sorts of*
> *havoc in your bodies and lives.*
>
> *You have been taught that some emotions are good*
> *and some are bad. Fear and anger you try to clamp*
> *down, but unexpressed they become shadows,*
> *which follow you everywhere longing to be felt and*
> *released. When joy comes dancing by, you sip, and*
> *it begins to open you. In opening yourselves to joy,*
> *you let all the other emotions in as well. In doing*
> *so, you feel anger at what you see around you. You*
> *become afraid so you shut it all down. And joy*
> *moves on without you. You blame the joy for*
> *leaving you. You call it fleeting. You say that you*
> *cannot trust it. And so you put it further from*
> *yourself.*

*We tell you now, that you will never be happy. You will never be satisfied or content. You will never be at peace until you open to and follow joy.*

*And yes, you may be flooded with many emotions. But floods are temporary, Beloveds. They move through with great force but they leave ground that is rich and fertile. And you will find that when you let your emotions run freely and acknowledge them, they will no longer have the power to incapacitate you. That is not their purpose.*

*Emotions have been given as tools to guide you on your path. Fear tells you to pause, to wait and consider before making a choice. Fear is your ally. Welcome fear's wisdom. Anger impassions you. It is a strong fire, and lets you know when something is vitally important. But you have to face it, to feel it in order to understand what it is telling you. Discontent, envy, jealousy – these too are your allies. They let you know when it is time to make change, to look deeper, to give yourself the things you need. But how do you know what you truly need?*

*My Beloveds, this is where Joy comes in. Joy is an ally to help you remember your soul purpose and to help you find and follow the path that will take you to meet it. Joy is one of the Creator's brilliant designs. Today, you might call it an "app" like a GPS for your life path. It will tell you to move ahead, turn left, slow down, reroute… but first you have to load it and learn how to use it.*

*Begin by simply noticing when you experience even a moment of joy. Memorize the feeling and begin to look for more of it. It is not difficult to find: it is everywhere. But you have to train yourself to see it.*

*You cannot feel joy from your head. You cannot think it into being. Joy is a feeling, and you will feel it very specifically in your body. Notice where you feel it. That's where the "app" is loaded. Yes, it's very close to where you have loaded fear or anger or many other emotions. Stay focused on the joy, feed it by simply remembering the moment that brought it. A joyful moment may be fleeting, but its memory is forever.*

*Joy is not always a loud emotion, but it is a very strong one. It is stronger than fear, anger, sorrow and rage.*

*Joy can infuse fear – like when you really want to do something, but it's scary. When you let the joy run along side of the fear, joy will overtake it. Fear is not interested in staying around. Fear simply wants to be heard. Hear the message of fear and follow the joy.*

*Joy tempers anger. Anger (and rage) want action: they are hungry fires. Joy focuses the energy of that fire into right action. Follow joy with the fire of your anger or rage. Remember that the anger and*

63

rage are a response to joy being diminished in some way that you cannot allow. You are not angry for example at an injustice – you are angry that justice (and the joy represented by it) has been thwarted or diminished. When things are "right" in your world, you feel joy.

Hatred is very destructive because it always harms the soul. It is a lack in emotion and a sign of impotence. It weakens and lessens you. Even still, it serves you in that it tells you that you have strayed very far from your path. You have missed the lessons that life has brought to you, and you are endangering not only yourself, but also those around you. Hatred is the emptying out of your emotional tool bag. It is a denial of the sacred and the joy in all. When you cannot see hope in someone else, you cannot see it in yourself. Do not listen to hatred. Turn from it. Seek immediate help, so that you may find your way back to your soul path.

Sorrow is the passing of joy, a very specific joy. With experience, you learn that while sorrow releases one joy it opens the way for new joy. And again, with experience you will learn that even in the moments of devastation when joy passes but new joys have not yet entered, there is a cleansing that happens. This cleansing opens your capacity for joy, love and happiness.

Your particular joy is unique to you, and it is keyed into your soul purpose. If followed it will lead you to your life path. Be aware that there is more than

*one path to fulfilling your life purpose. Never fear
that you will lose it. We should say never fear that
it will lose you. You may indeed lose track of it.
You may get distracted by many things, including
someone else's joy. But your allies -
discontentment, envy, jealousy, fear and even anger
- will tell you that you've lost your way. And when
you look, when you once again remember to feel and
follow your joy, the path will once again be under
your feet.*

*We cannot too strongly tell you of the importance
of joy. It will change your life – rather it will help
you find your true life. Do not fear joy or the other
emotions that will dance with it. It is one of your
most powerful tools. When you follow yours, others
will see and begin to have the courage to follow
theirs. When you follow joy, you will learn how
beautifully it grounds you in your soul purpose.
You will see how the Universe conspires with you
to help you meet that purpose.*

*May joy both lead and follow you, Beloveds."*

As we learn to court joy and build our capacity to
experience joy, we can also learn ways to amplify joy
and to wield joy as a tool of transformation. Sound
and gratitude are two specific ways of both
amplifying our own experience of joy and using joy

as a tool of transformation. These will be discussed in the next chapter.

Personal Reflection

Joy is affected by and informs our other emotions. Take a look at the list of emotions in Appendix A. How familiar/comfortable are you with them?

Notice which ones create the strongest feeling in you. Particularly notice any emotion that you find yourself not wanting to feel or ones you believe you "shouldn't" feel.

Here is an exercise in empowering your emotional intelligence and in discovering your own capacity to feel. Use the list of emotions and insert different ones into this statement:

*"As a human I have a natural ability to feel (insert emotion). I can experience this without judgment knowing that it is not what I feel that defines me. It is my ability to appropriately express what I feel that will define me. '*

# Techniques that Support Joy

Although joy is a natural emotion that we all come into the world knowing how to feel, we've forgotten how to let it in. This section is all about how to learn to flow naturally with joy again. It's important to recognize that I am not teaching you to be in joy. I am helping you remember how. These simple and very easy to incorporate techniques will be, well, joyful. So don't look at this as work, look at these exercises as the tickets to joy. You've already paid the price, now take the ride!

## "Forest Bathing"

A friend introduced me to the phrase "Forest Bathing." It is easiest to understand if we compare it to hiking in a forest with the intention of getting to the top of the trail. We stay focused on our feet and on conquering the trail. We usually do this with a sense of needing to speed through it. But what if instead, we walked the trail with an awareness of the actual forest we're walking through? What if we slowed down, made less noise and welcomed the inhabitants of the forest to be in communion with us? Now, I'm not talking about walking in the wilderness and inviting bears to come dance with us. I'm inviting us to walk through the forest with the same intention we might have sun bathing on a beach. We are not just lying on the beach when we're sun bathing. We're asking the sun to shine upon us and bless us with the warmth and beauty of its rays. We are inhaling, even ingesting the sun. Doesn't it feel grand, particularly after a long winter? Try it in a forest. Breathe it in. Open yourself to its beauty. Open to forest bathing. Here's a way to start:

The following technique is best learned out in nature and can easily be incorporated into a short walk. Begin your walk with conscious breathing. Become aware of your physicality - your feet, hands, legs, arms, trunk, neck, head, shoulders, hips, ... Allow yourself to enJOY the movement of your body, the flow of breath through the body, the inhale of oxygen and the exhale of carbon dioxide.

As you continue, be aware that while you are inhaling oxygen and releasing carbon dioxide with your exhale, the plants around you are inhaling your carbon dioxide and releasing oxygen. We breathe together. We rely on each other for our very breath.

As you continue on your walk, let your awareness of this connection deepen.

Now, allow yourself to notice the beauty around you. Focus on one particular plant and simply admire its beauty. In the silence of your heart tell it how beautiful it is. Love it. Let your admiration shine from your eyes and heart. Drink in the beauty, take in as much as you like.

Let yourself notice that as you admire the plant it responds by becoming even more beautiful. Notice that it begins to offer that beauty to you with its exhale. And as you inhale, drinking in the beauty, you become more beautiful. Share that beauty in your exhale.

This is very much like falling in love. The object/person before you is beautiful in your eyes. Your attentions and the love you offer affects both of you. It is a system. We are all connected. We are connected by the breath on the physical level. And when we allow ourselves to celebrate that connection we automatically breathe together – we conspire. We don't have to think about this. We simply have to open to its magic.

By the way, as you are breathing and sharing beauty with a tree or a rose or even a blade of grass, you are bringing your energy field into balance. Your Chakras (energy centers in your body) move into more balance. Your immune system is boosted. You become more vibrant. The plant does too.

This is very easy to do. It will bring you as much joy as you can take in. And that joy will radiate back out to the Universe. This is a powerful healing practice. It is something you can do everyday. You will be amazed at how quickly you can step into this practice. You can love a plant in your office while waiting on hold for a call. You can send beauty and joy to a tree while you wait for the stoplight to turn green. You can love an entire coffee shop of people while you wait for your order to be filled.

There are so many benefits to doing this for you and for all around you. It will keep you in the present. It will lower your blood pressure and your stress. It will magnetize love and joy into your life. It will help banish the fear that seems so prevalent in our culture. Try it once a day for one week. Make that commitment, and you'll see the benefits for yourself.

**Gratitude**

As Dr. Brené Brown tells us, a practice of gratitude is the key to opening to joy (see page 23). Please, do not make this difficult. Stay in the wonder of it. Play in gratitude. Here's a few easy ways to do it:

*Gratitude Journal* – When you feel grateful, write in a journal why. Use details so that when you read it you can touch into the feelings. Pick a time in your day to sit for a moment, consider what you are grateful for, and write it down. I like to keep the journal close, so when I notice the gratitude I can record it. Then when you're feeling low, afraid, alone… you can go to the gratitude journal and remember all that you are grateful for.

I like to think of gratitude as an indication to the Universe that you can receive more abundance. It's like when a small child wants a dog. Many parents will start with a fish. If the child can successfully care for the fish, then they talk about the possibility of a dog. I do not use this analogy to suggest that the Universe is testing us. But if we are unable to show gratitude for what we do have, how can the Universe know that we are ready for more?

The practice of gratitude reaps all kinds of benefits. It taps into joy and opens you to possibilities. It feels really good. It stimulates the flow of abundance.

*Daily Gratitude* – There are many ways to move into a daily gratitude practice. Some families share their gratitude over dinner. It helps us to reflect on our day and to communicate in a positive way what's happening in our lives. This sharing connects us to each other in a unique and life affirming way. You can also do this practice one-on-one with each member of the family as you tuck them in for bed. My favorite version of this is to start my day with daily gratitude for the opportunities that lie ahead. I'm very specific. For example, "I am grateful for the opportunity to work with a new client today" or "I am thankful that I will spend time with a dear friend over dinner." This "pre-loading" of gratitude sets the tone and intention of my day. I am more likely to have a great session with the new client and to have a wonderful time with my friend. I also end my day with gratitude, reflecting on the gifts I have received throughout the day. I do this right before going to sleep. It tends to quiet my mind and relax my body.

**River Song**

Years ago, I moved to my ancestral lands in northwest Ohio. I went because a dream led me to go. In the first months of being there I discovered that in order to open a massage practice I would have to go back to school. As I was already moving toward other healing work, I chose not to do that. I expected that I would be reconnecting with all my relatives that still lived in the area, but found that only a few welcomed me.

My dream had called and in it the Ancestors had told me "we know you, but you don't know us. Feed this land." I was doing everything I could think of to do just that, and not feeling like I was very successful. One day, I was feeling particularly low, and I went to the river and sat against a tree near Independence Dam.

I have always had a sense of connection with nature and knew that some form of communication happened when you paid attention. But on this day I learned so much more is possible.

I sat against the tree feeling sorry for myself and very much alone. I mumbled something like, "You don't know us, we know you – huh! No one even remembers me here." And from deep within the tree I heard him say, "I remember you."

As I leaned into him, the tree showed me a scene from my childhood. I was only about seven-years-old and we were at a family reunion. The entire family was gathered around the picnic tables and I had wandered over to this tree. I was singing and dancing around it and having a great time.

The people I belonged to were over there but I felt more at home by myself with the tree. To be remembered by the tree seemed a great honor. I was overwhelmed by it and I began to sob. Once I started crying I couldn't stop. All my fears, doubts and loneliness just flowed out through the tears. I felt held by the tree. He witnessed my pain without any judgment.

I emptied myself and then came to that quiet place after the storm. I let myself truly rest in the arms of the tree. As I sat in that peace, I began to hear a very quiet song. I listened deeper. It was a voice, not a bird or other animal. The song was weak, and I could barely hear it. Tree told me to sing the song back to itself. I did. As I sang, the song grew stronger, and I became aware that it was coming from the river.

The song continued, and I became aware that the Angels were with us. They explained what was happening.

"The song you hear is the innate song of the river – before it was dammed and its power harnessed for man's purposes. The river has been damaged and polluted, but always the innate song remains. When you listen and hear it, you become a witness to the river's innate self. When you sing its song back to it, you remind it of its true nature. Feel how it grows. Feel its strength returning. "

I smiled and felt the joy of serving in this way. I continued singing with the river, and I began to notice that I too felt stronger. My singing had shifted into my own song. The river and I were now serving each other, both growing stronger, both healing. It was wonderful!

"There are three rivers that feed this land," Angels said. "Sing them. Sing each of them at least once each week. Learn *RiverSong*. It is what you were called here to do."

I sang the rivers each week for several months. When I no longer needed to work at focusing and it became easy, I began receiving dreams that called me back to Washington State.

Although I continue to call it *RiverSong,* I have applied the same technique to working with plants, animals, people, landscapes and more. Everything has an innate song. When the song is witnessed and reflected back, the memory of who/what we are is activated. This remembering calls to us and we begin to heal ourselves. In the magic of this process, we call others to their innate song.

The Angels tell me this is an ancient healing technique – very powerful and much needed in our world.

## Sound

Sound is a powerful force in the world, and we should become more aware of the sounds we subject ourselves to. There are a growing number of sound healers. These are folks, like myself, dedicated to healing through sound. Many of the techniques are really quite easy and do not require special talents to incorporate into our lives.

Toning is one of the easiest techniques. Quite simply you open your mouth and let a tone come out. If it feels or sounds shaky, sound a bit louder and that will most likely go away.

IMPORTANT! Toning is not about sounding pretty or sounding good. It is simply about sounding. The particular tone that moves through you is the perfect tone for you at the time. Trust it.

Breathe, open and tone. When you're out of breath, breathe, open and tone again. If the tone changes, that's OK. When toning, you are shifting the energies in your body and around you. As they shift, the tone may also shift. Allow it.
Sound the tone. Hear the tone. Take in the sound, and let it flow through your body. Do this for several minutes or much longer if you wish.

## "AH"

When you tone to the "ah" sound (as in alleluia) you will be accessing the heart Chakra.

## "OO"

When you tone to the "oo" sound (as in soup) you tend to access the lower Chakras.

### "EE"
When you tone to the "ee" sound (as in peep) you tend to access the upper Chakras.

You can do a lot with simple toning, and you can learn advanced toning techniques. But start with these simple techniques, and see where it takes you. Notice how you feel before you begin, and how you feel after.

Sound, especially toning, can help you move through and process emotion. It can clear your energy fields at the end of a long day. It can dispel tension in your body and in your environment. It can be a powerful tool to healing, and it can open you to a greater capacity for joy.

## Being Silly: It Won't Kill You

If you're thinking that toning, breathing with trees and well, being joyful, will make you feel silly, you may be right. Being silly won't kill you. However, stress probably will!

One of my teachers posed this question:

> Imagine that you have just come off a freeway ramp and are at a stoplight. It's late at night. On the side of the road to your left is a person sitting in fetal position and crying and sobbing. She is clearly in a great deal of despair. On the right side of the road a second person is doubled over laughing so hard that tears are running down her face. Who are you most afraid of?

Most people will say the person laughing makes them more uncomfortable and even frightened. Despair is more common to us than laughter.

I dated a man several years ago. He was very involved politically and environmentally. He was drawn to me because we shared music, and I am in great joy when doing music. One night, he suggested we watch a movie. My hopes for a quiet romantic evening were dashed when he brought a documentary with Al Gore and others talking about the crisis we were in on our planet.

After the movie, he turned to me and asked what I thought. I told him it was a well made movie, but that none of it was new information to me. I will never forget the fury on his face when he asked, "You know about this?" It was followed by an accusatory glare when he demanded, "How can you be so happy?!!!"

I was as stunned as he was. I calmly looked at him and said, "Joy and happiness is my chosen response. This crisis we are in has been caused by people in fear, people wanting more power, people who are angry. The problems were created in the field of fear and anger. I am choosing not to feed that field of fear and anger. I am choosing to find what is good and beautiful in the world. I am choosing happiness and joy. This is an active and I think a powerful response to these crises."

This is not always an easy path, but then neither is the path he chose in response. I believe that I have the most power to change the world within myself, in my neighborhood and in my community. So I spend my energies there rather than dwelling on global issues. He assumed that I must be ignorant of what was happening in the world. I assured him that I am not.

Being an empath, intuitive and psychic, I am aware of what's going on around me intensely. If I did not choose to feed joy and happiness, I would drown in sorrow, pain and suffering. Like many others, I would probably turn to alcohol, drugs or prescribed medications to numb myself.

I actively choose song, sounding and natural beauty to counter the destructive forces in the world. It puts my life in perspective and helps keep my thoughts positively powerful.

## Personal Reflection

This chapter has had enough reflection in it. However, I encourage you to ask yourself how you approached these exercises - with wonder and ease, with resistance,... ? If you made it hard work, I invite you to return and choose an exercise that feels easy and playful. Start there, return to the others when you can do so with the same ease and playfulness.

# The Joy Brigade

I suggest we each take the research, stories and the techniques I have offered in this book seriously. Let's become the Joy Brigade pouring buckets of joy on the destructive forces around us.

Before I proceed with this idea, I want to remind us that emotions are simply emotions. Fear and anger are not innately negative. They are our allies when we use them well. When we do not attend to them *or* when we over focus on them, we experience negative affects. These emotions access our flight or fight branch of the nervous system. They narrow our focus to base survival and shut down our creative centers. This is indeed a very positive thing when you are in immediate physical danger. You need to be focused on survival.

Emotions such as joy, happiness and contentment access other parts of our nervous system and encourage a diffuse focus with relaxation and rest leading to the increased abilities that Dr. Frederickson detailed.

Culturally, we tend to over focus on fear and anger. They have become negative forces in our world. But we can shift this power. Psychological and spiritual experts tell us positive thinking is more powerful than negative thinking. One bucket of joy will counter many buckets of fear and anger. As the Angels tell us, JOY is more powerful.

Physicist Gregg Braden tells us that it only takes the square root of 1% of the population to create change. I'll do the math for you. In a group of 100,000, it takes only 31.6 people to make a change. You can be one of the 31.6 people in your community. Everyone benefits, first of all you!

## Drink in Joy

I was driving home one day, and I noticed two small children running out into a parking lot. They had that "we're finally free" look about them you usually see as the final school bell rings. And right behind them was a man, who I assume was their father. He had the same look about him. As they approached their car, they shared a smile and a sense of anticipation. I suspected that a well deserved trip to Baskin and Robbins was ahead of them.

I found myself looking away so as not to intrude on their moment. But then I realized I was absolutely not taking anything from them by my observation. In fact, I was participating in their joy. They sparked my joy, and I knew I would carry it with me and probably spark someone else's joy. Even in this moment of writing about the incident I feel that same joy. I refuse to let that joy be fleeting. I took it in. I drank from their joy and expanded it. I carry it with me still.

Let's open ourselves to these moments. Let's soak them up and gather them in and pour their healing nectar out into the world.

Let us be the Joy Brigade – like a fire brigade saving a house from fire. Instead of buckets of water, we will carry buckets of joy. Instead of saving a house, we will save ourselves, our neighborhoods, our community, our world.

Joy is a renewable resource*. It easily expands. When our joy is met with disapproval or suspicion, let us see that as a sign that joy is indeed needed in our world.

When I was in college, my mother came to visit. One of my friends told her that I got drunk every weekend. The truth was that I rarely drank more than one drink and usually didn't drink at all. The night before this incident someone offered me a beer, and several people in the room told them I didn't drink. I accepted the beer but certainly was not drunk. When I asked the friend why she told my mother I was drunk every weekend, she said it was because I was always singing and dancing down the hall. She couldn't believe that someone would do that unless they were drunk. I re-educated her.

I have been overlooked for academic and corporate jobs because I was too joyful and happy. I understand that the world is indeed suspicious when faced with joy and happiness. They so often see it as a lack of ability to be serious or to be credible. I can be both seriously joyful and joyfully serious. I can happily sit with someone on his/her death bed or in the hospital. It brings me joy to be able to be a witness to these significant life moments. I have learned to be more circumspect with physical expressions of my joy – like dancing and singing down the halls. I've learned to carry a quieter and more grounded joy.

I admit that in the process of that, I inhibited my joy as I learned to conform. Now I see that I did not need to inhibit it, but to simply appropriately express it. I am committed to not only following my joy but to drinking more deeply of it.

Join me. Grab a bucket or even a cupful of joy, and share it with the world. Allow yourself to notice the sources of joy around you. Drink them in. Fortify yourself. Heal yourself. Join the Joy Brigade!

Personal Reflection

I invite you to choose 1 - 3 ways in which you will allow joy to flow in the following week. You can commit to doing something that you know brings you joy. You can commit to allowing your joy even if someone tries to squelch it. You can commit to noticing joy in others and expanding it by taking it in and sharing the joy.

# Follow Joy. Don't Chase It.

Remember that we live in a world of extreme sports, taste explosions and a general habit of believing that things need to be big and fast. We're told to go get "it," work hard and never stop. So you may find yourself chasing joy – going after it like some conquest. You might be tempted to seek it in foreign countries, in your bucket list or in other places outside of your usual realm.

Here me now! Joy is everywhere. Joy wants to dance with you. Joy is continually tapping you on the shoulder or winking at you across the room. Joy is like a lover that simply wants to be with you and share your life.

Give it some room to move into your life. Clean out a metaphorical drawer for it to leave a few essentials with you because there will be times when you will not be able to feel joy. There will be times when other emotions will crowd it out. And when it returns to you, you will appreciate it even more.

Chasing joy is a waste of your resources. It's like standing in a pristine meadow and leaving it to find air or beauty. Just inhale. Open to the sources of joy all around you. If you cannot find joy in your environment, you will not be able to find and hold it anywhere else for any significant time.

Having said that, I want to acknowledge that occasionally we lose perspective, and it can be helpful to go on retreat, to get away and clear your head, to experience a change of scenery. Definitely allow this in your life. However, if that's the only way you can experience joy, it's time for some change.

If other emotions are consistently crowding out joy, they are probably telling you something really important. Listen. Then remember to tap into joy through a short trip or through pulling out old memories. Remember joy. Memorize how it feels. This will call it to you and then you can follow it to a place or situation that will be better suited for you. Never let anyone – including yourself - tell you that you don't deserve or are not capable of joy.

If you find yourself singing or thinking that there is "more joy somewhere," know that you are holding joy away from you. The surest way to be in joy is to open to it right where you are, to celebrate it right now – *even if it feels small.* Once you open to it and allow it to flow, you can follow it to a deeper pool.

Photo by Lisa Langel

FYI: When you move to a deeper pool of joy and wade in it, you will increase your capacity for joy. When this happens, sometimes that deep pool begins to feel shallow. The pool has not changed. You have. The river of joy flows into ever deepening pools. Just keep following it.

Here's the last point I want to make about following joy: following joy does not require moving physically. I want to be certain you do not interpret this as a need to leave where you are and go somewhere else in a physical sense. The ever-deepening pools of joy are actually within you. What inspires or triggers that joy may be outside of you.

To understand this more specifically, I invite you to do the following exercise.
Sit with something that appeals to you. This something can be a new born baby, an ocean view, a puppy, a hot rod, a vat of melted chocolate or someone you adore. As you look at this appealing sight, notice that warm or soft feeling inside you. Yep, that something in you that makes you want to smile just being in its presence. Notice the feeling. Now let yourself feel it more. Let the feeling expand. Don't limit it. Don't time it. Just be with it, and let it become as big and deep as it wants to be. Now you are following joy.

Here's an advanced version. You are going to do exactly the same thing. But this time, before you start the process, look around and notice your environment. Then go ahead and absorb yourself in your something special. Let it grow and expand. When you feel full, look around you again and notice the environment. It probably looks different. The colors and light may be more intense or brighter. You are in a field of joy, and it changes how you perceive your world. And believe me, it actually changes your world. It flows from you to everything around you. By the way, that special something doesn't have to literally be in front of you. You can bring it to you with a thought. Imagine it.

**Ultimate Permission**

One of my intentions in writing this book was to give people permission to be in joy. I want to be a voice for celebrating our lives deeply and for not just allowing, but actively engaging in the joy of the world around us and within us.

I give you permission! Dip your toe in. Wade in. Submerge yourself. The water is good.

Know this. I can give you all the permission in the world. The ultimate permission, however, must come from you. Gift it to yourself. Do it silently. Do it in the privacy of your own home or in the shower, if you're feeling shy about it. As you gain experience and calibrate yourself to feel and allow more and more joy, you may sing it from the roof tops. Do it at your pace and comfort. Without your permission, joy will never be a powerful force in your life. Only you can give the ultimate permission.

Personal Reflection

This chapter includes self-reflection. I invite you to take the exercise offered above and make it an active practice in your life..

Notes:

# Appendix A: List of Emotions

Too often in my work I hear clients voice an initial inability to know their own emotions. When I ask them how they do feel or how they want to feel, they say things like, "I want to feel that I have no debt." I then need to ask them how they will feel when they have no debt. Many clients stare at me for a few moments. I hold the silence so that they can imagine being debt free and then tap into the actual emotions they experience. Once they identify the emotion it becomes an ally and an empowering force for their intentions.

Below you will find a list of emotions. This is not intended to be complete, but rather to initiate a consciousness about the range and breadth of emotions that are available to us.

| | | |
|---|---|---|
| OPEN | HAPPY | ALIVE |
| UNDERSTANDING | GREAT | PLAYFUL |
| CONFIDENT | GLEEFUL | COURAGEOUS |
| RELIABLE | JOYOUS | ENERGETIC |
| FREE | LUCKY | LIBERATED |
| AMAZED | FORTUNATE | OPTIMISTIC |
| SYMPATHETIC | OVERJOYED | IMPULSIVE |
| INTERESTED | THANKFUL | VITAL |
| RECEPTIVE | FESTIVE | THRILLED |
| ACCEPTING | ECSTATIC | WONDERFUL |
| KIND | GLAD | AROUSED |
| SUNNY | CHEERFUL | ELATED |
| CALM | PEACEFUL | SURPRISED |
| PLEASED | ENCOURAGED | SERENE |
| RELAXED | BRIGHT | BLESSED |
| REASSURED | CREATIVE | CONTENT |

| | | |
|---|---|---|
| LOVING | CONCERNED | EAGER |
| CONSIDERATE | FASCINATED | KEEN |
| EARNEST | AFFECTIONATE | TENDER |
| INTRIGUED | ANXIOUS | DETERMINED |
| ENTHUSIASTIC | BOLD | BRAVE |
| CHALLENGED | OPTIMISTIC | PASSIONATE |
| WARM | TOUCHED | CLOSE |
| LOVED | COMFORTED | HOPEFUL |
| CONFIDENT | DARING | EXCITED |
| INTENT | INQUISITIVE | FASCINATED |
| STRONG | SURE | FREE |
| CERTAIN | REBELLIOUS | DRAMATIC |
| DYNAMIC | TENACIOUS | HARDY |
| SECURE | IMPULSIVE | HELPLESS |
| ALONE | PARALYZED | FATIGUED |
| USELESS | INFERIOR | SUPERIOR |
| PERPLEXED | CONFUSED | DISILLUSIONED |
| SLY | EMPTY | FRUSTRATED |
| WOEFUL | TRAGIC | DOMINATED |
| UNEASY | UNSURE | STUPEFIED |
| RAGEFUL | INDECISIVE | LOST |
| PESSIMISTIC | TENSE | LONELY |
| IRRITATED | ANGRY | DISAPPOINTED |
| ASHAMED | FEARFUL | GUILTY |
| DIMINISHED | MISERABLE | AGGRESSIVE |
| INFLAMED | INCENSED | IN DESPAIR |
| SULKY | PROVOKED | BITTER |
| RESENTFUL | CROSS | HATEFUL |
| ANNOYED | HOSTILE | POWERLESS |

| | | |
|---|---|---|
| POWERFUL | LOUSY | UPSET |
| WEARY | WARY | LIFELESS |
| DULL | SUSPICIOUS | TERRIFIED |
| PAINED | INJURED | DEJECTED |
| TORMENTED | OFFENDED | FRIGHTENED |
| RESTLESS | HEARTBROKEN | AGONIZED |
| HUMILIATED | ALIENATED | COWARDLY |
| SCARED | NERVOUS | CRUSHED |
| SAD | SORROWFUL | GRIEF |
| UNHAPPY | DESPERATE | DISMAYED |
| MOURNFUL | TEARFUL | REJECTED |

# A ppendix B: Inspirations

I have included a few of my favorite inspirational writings on joy to help you seed and tend to your own life of joy. May it be blessed and overflowing. ~ C. Rhalena

\*\*\*

"People who report that they are happy have a common trait: they actively connect with friends and loved ones for an hour or two a day." ~ Deepak Chopra

If you knew yourself for even one moment, if you could just glimpse your most beautiful face, maybe you wouldn't slumber so deeply in that house of clay.

Why not move into your house of joy and shine into every crevice! For you are the secret Treasure-bearer, and always have been. Didn't you know? ~ Rumi

Keep knocking, and the joy inside will eventually open up a window and look out to see who's there. ~ Rumi

"Anything is one of a million paths. Therefore you must always keep in mind that a path is only a path; if you feel you should not follow it, you must not stay with it under any conditions. To have such clarity you must lead a disciplined life. Only then will you know that any path is only a path and there is no affront, to oneself or to others, in dropping it if that is what your heart tells you to do. But your decision to keep on the path or to leave it must be free of fear or ambition. I warn you. Look at every path closely and deliberately.

Try it as many times as you think necessary.

This question is one that only a very old man asks. Does this path have a heart? All paths are the same: they lead nowhere. They are paths going through the forest, or into the forest. In my own life I could say I have traversed long long paths, but I am not anywhere. Does this path have a heart? If it does, the path is good; if it doesn't, it is of no use. Both paths lead nowhere; but one has a heart, the other doesn't. One makes for a joyful journey; as long as you follow it, you are one with it. The other will make you curse your life. One makes you strong; the other weakens you.

Before you embark on any path ask the question: Does this path have a heart? If the answer is no, you will know it, and then you must choose another path. The trouble is nobody asks the question; and when a man finally realizes that he has taken a path without a heart, the path is ready to kill him. At that point very few men can stop to deliberate, and leave the path. A path without a heart is never enjoyable. You have to work hard even to take it. On the other hand, a path with heart is easy; it does not make you work at liking it."
~ Carlos Castaneda

"When you make a choice, you change the future."
~ Deepak Chopra

Photo by Suzy Wenger

## Tripping Over Joy

What is the difference
Between your experience of existence
And that of a saint?

The saint knows
That the spiritual path
Is a sublime chess game with God

And that the beloved
Has just made such a fantastic move
That the saint is now continually
Tripping over Joy
And bursting out in laughter
And saying, "I surrender!"

Whereas, my dear,
I am afraid you still think
You have a thousand serious moves."
~ Hafiz, *I Heard God Laughing: Poems of Hope and Joy*

Photo by Suzy Wenger

## Strange Miracle

O Wondrous creatures,
By what strange miracle
Do you so often
Not smile?"
~ Hafiz, *I Heard God Laughing: Poems of Hope and Joy*

## You Don't Have to Act Crazy Anymore

"You don't have to act crazy anymore—
We all know you were good at that,

Now retire, my dear,
From all that hard work you do
Of bringing pain to your sweet eyes and heart.

Look in a clear mountain mirror
See the beautiful ancient warrior
And the divine elements
You always carry inside
That infused this universe with sacred life
So long ago"

~ Hafiz, *I Heard God Laughing: Poems of Hope and Joy*

"When you do things from your soul, you feel a
river moving in you, a joy." ~ Rumi

"Remember to light the candle of joy daily and all the gloom will disappear from your life."

~ Djwhal Khul


"You have to sniff out joy. Keep your nose to the joy trail." ~ Buffy Sainte-Marie


"What I know for sure is that you feel real JOY in direct proportion to how connected you are to living your truth." ~ Oprah


"When we are centered in joy, we attain our wisdom." ~ Marianne Williamson


"Release the joy that is inside of another, and you release the joy that is inside of you." ~ *Neal Donald Walch*


## On Joy and Sorrow

Your joy is your sorrow unmasked.

And the selfsame well from which your laughter rises was oftentimes filled with your tears.

And how else can it be?

The deeper that sorrow carves into your being, the more joy you can contain.

Is not the cup that holds your wine the very cup

that was burned in the potter's oven?

And is not the lute that soothes your spirit, the very wood that was hollowed with knives?

When you are joyous, look deep into your heart and you shall find it is only that which has given you sorrow that is giving you joy.

When you are sorrowful look again in your heart, and you shall see that in truth you are weeping for that which has been your delight.


Some of you say, "Joy is greater than sorrow," and others say, "Nay, sorrow is the greater."

But I say unto you, they are inseparable.

Together they come, and when one sits alone with you at your board, remember that the other is asleep upon your bed.

Verily you are suspended like scales between your sorrow and your joy.

Only when you are empty are you at a standstill and balanced.

When the treasure-keeper lifts you to weigh his gold and his silver, needs must your joy or your sorrow rise or fall.

~ Kahlil Gibran


"If you try to get rid of fear and anger without knowing their meaning, they will grow stronger and return."

~ Deepak Chopra

"We need Joy as we need air. We need Love as we need water. We need each other as we need the earth we share." ~ *Maya Angelou*


"Rise, rise, rise. Let your devotion guide your way.
Soar and you will fly, each and every day.
Sing your heart open and wide, like the sky.
Plant your feet on the earth below, you are alive!"

~ Susan Chiat (chant from her CD, *From the Heart*
http://www.cdbaby.com/cd/susanchiat)

Photo by Elizabeth Dobes

# Joy, Born in Fear
A short teaching story

The soul called Kestrel floated about the Universe in absolute joy. Shining big or small, it didn't matter. The light from Kestrel was strong and vibrant. She loved moving among the planets and feeling how her light changed as each one called forth a different response from her. And when she danced with the stars her light became part of their song.

Lately, Kestrel most often found herself near the planet Earth. It was a beautiful planet, and she particularly delighted in dancing with the Northern Lights. When she got that close to Earth, her soul tears flowed freely and her light pulsed stronger than usual. Something was calling Kestrel to Earth, and so she decided that it was once again time for her to incarnate.

Uriel, the Archangel, knew Kestrel had forgotten the pain and fear that was so rampant on Earth. He couldn't quite remember how many lives she'd spent on that planet, but he knew each time was hard on her. Yet Kestrel's soul seemed to have an affinity for it even though in Uriel's mind Earth seemed to beat her up. She always returned so weak from living in a place of such fear. As she started to heal from her times on Earth, she'd forget the hardships; her natural joy simply left no room for such memories.

Then once again Earth's need called, and Kestrel willingly answered. She'd get a far away look in her eyes and with determination say, "Joy must be shared or at least offered as an option to fear."

Now Kestrel waited in the ethers outside of Uriel's home. She needed his guidance and help with the details of this incarnation. But Uriel needed a bit of time to put aside his concern for her. She'd made her decision and experience taught him she'd never change her mind. The best he could do for her was to support her in every way he knew how.

So Uriel stayed for a short time inside his home at the heart of the Universe. It was an interesting place. Visually it seemed to be made of marble with several large columns and lots of marble benches. Many beings seemed to need to see him as strong and solid. So when they came to him he gave them the comfort of seeing lasting strength.

But Uriel was wise enough to know that strength came from a significant degree of flexibility. So at first glance the marble looked solid and unchangeable, but soon it would morph, shifting slowly between the softest hues of pinks, yellows and greens. The first time someone sat on one of the cold looking marble benches, they were surprised. The bench was warm and seemed to soften as if to welcome them in. Their sighs at this sensation both delighted and intrigued him. Some said it reminded them of sitting on their grandmother's lap.

Today he wanted something charming to make Kestrel smile. Uriel waved his hand creating a glowing lotus with translucent pink petals floating in a gently bubbling fountain of delicately scented water. With a smile, he added a green frog spitting a stream of water into the air, which cascaded down in a tinkling song. Pink and green were great colors for balancing the heart Chakra, he thought to himself. Uriel knew his creation was as much for his comfort as Kestrel's, and it gave him the answer he was looking for. He would welcome Kestrel with a balanced heart and send her to Earth with gifts that would help her keep hers balanced while she was there.

He now moved to where Kestrel waited. They simply took each other in for a moment. Wordless, their eyes said everything. Love, compassion and deep joy pulsed from and between them. It was such a delicious feeling – better than the most satisfying hug in the corporal worlds. They took their fill and then moved to the marble bench by the lotus fountain. Kestrel trailed her fingers through the water and patted the frog on the head in greeting.

With a gentle touch on her 3rd eye, Uriel renewed Kestrel's memory of Earth and how it operated. Although she had been there many times, her

memories faded when she returned home to her
natural form of soft shifting light and peaceful sound.
Uriel watched now as a tremor moved through
Kestrel. Her light grew deeper and a minute tone of
sadness entered her eyes. It pained his heart to
witness this shift.

"Where would you like to go this time?" Uriel softly
asked.

"I've been considering this ever since I made my
decision to return to Earth. I've decided I would like
to be female. I want to be birthed into a family that
has potential for great love but has trouble accessing
it. And I would like to be in a place that does not
suffer great hardship. Perhaps a quiet town in a place
where e110veryone can have what they need
relatively easily," Kestrel began.

"And what would you like to learn or experience on
this visit," Uriel asked?

"I want to know what it's like to use my gifts very
well to help heal this fearful planet. Oh, and music
please. I've got to have my music. Of course, I wish to
radiate joy."

Uriel chuckled. "My dear, you would not be you in
any form if you did not radiate joy. That is a given."

She nodded in acknowledgment. "I want to do it
powerfully this time, Uriel. I need to understand why
fear is so tantalizing when it can be so painful. I think

it would help me to understand joy more fully. It's easy for me to just emit joy without any need for understanding. This time I'd like to emit joy and understand its power."

"Very well," Uriel said with a smile.
"And this time I would like to remember my life here, and its expansive possibilities," Kestrel added.

Uriel shook his head, and a tear slid down his cheek. "No dear, you cannot wish for that."

"Oh, but I do wish for that. I want you to trust me in this, for I am certain that this is indeed what I need to do." Kestrel held Uriel's gaze as she spoke, so he could feel and see her true desire.

"Earth is not a playground," he reminded her. "This is a particularly challenging time on Earth. There are relatively few ascended masters living on the planet. It's a dark planet; people are lost and frightened."

"Yes, I know. I feel it," she said as a tear slid down her cheek. "Their need calls to me. I sense they are aware of the depth of their need and simply don't know what to do about it. I am willing to risk this. They need me."

"Very well," Uriel said. "Are you ready?"

"Yes," she smiled.

Enfolding her in his wings, Uriel kissed her crown and promised he would be with her.

***

Lucy Kruger left the doctor's office in a daze. Pregnant again? I'm not yet getting a good night's sleep with the baby I have now. How will I ever have the energy for another? And Carrie's birthing was so difficult. Split open and exhausted - barely healed from the episiotomy – they sent me home alone with a new baby and to a husband who I barely recognize anymore.

I don't want this baby, God. Why did you send me another? David can't stand the crying. I don't think he loves me anymore. He hits me. He screams at me to shut Carrie up. She's a baby. If he would calm down, so would she. I know you have a plan and you won't give me more than I can handle. But I don't know how I'm going to do this.

Her mind kept churning as she walked down the hall. David looked up as she came into the waiting room. She smiled as if the thought of having another child was like winning the lottery. She told him the news as they walked to the car. She cooed at the baby as she set her down and slid onto the car seat next to her. Lucy sighed as David shut the door.

How can she be so happy David wondered as he walked around the car to the driver's side? They nearly killed her having the last one. I can't stand to see her unhappy or in pain. Something seems to snap in me. I feel helpless.

The first pregnancy was bad enough and it went on for 10 months! She was so miserable and I couldn't do anything to help her. It made me mad, and I just took it out on her whenever she looked at me and I saw a tiny flicker of fear or hopelessness. What did she expect me to do? I can't carry the baby. And even if I could, she wouldn't let me. That's her job, "woman's work," she'd say.

All I can do is leave her alone – all alone, all day long – while I go to work to make money, so we can live in our small apartment that's about to get smaller. I've got to find a way to make things better and soon. And till then I'm shit out of luck.

They drove back to their small town in Iowa. As they passed the Woolworth's, David thought of stopping for a cherry coke - just to make the day special for her. But he didn't know how he was going to pay for today's doctor visit and milk for the baby as it was. Instead he slammed his hand against the steering wheel and cursed.

Lucy shivered. He never did this before they were married. She didn't know whether his outbursts would be the beginning of a full-blown rant or just a short flash of anger. Worse yet, she never knew what she did to make him so mad. It wasn't her fault she was pregnant again!

Why does she flinch in fear, David wondered. I'm not mad at her. I should keep my hands off of her instead of getting her pregnant. She can't get a good night's sleep with Carrie crying all the time and wanting to be fed and changed. She doesn't need *me* wanting her attentions. But then she touches my shoulder as she walks by my chair or puts her hand on my thigh as we settle in for the night. Does she just do that because she thinks it's her wifely duty? If I ask her, she just gets defensive. She won't tell me how to help her. And damn it, I should be able to feel frustrated and curse when I want to. He cursed again without even realizing it.

Lucy patted Carrie, more to comfort herself than the baby. God, please help him to keep his temper under control at Sherry's. The last thing I need is for my sisters and brothers to know he has such a temper. I couldn't stand for them to know the truth. They already don't like him. They feel sorry for me, but they don't know that at least now I have my own home and a place where I belong. I'm not working for someone else or cleaning up someone else's shit. This is my family, and they'll just have to get used to it.

She starts humming to the radio, and soon David is humming along too. The tension in the car lessens, and Lucy takes a breath of relief at the end of the song. As the next song begins, she turns and smiles at him looking like a woman who has everything she needs. David lowers his shoulders at the smile on her face. Instead of seeing it as a promise and an acknowledgment that they're in it together, he wonders how he will ever be able to keep that smile on her face and that look in her eyes. He knows he doesn't deserve it.

||||||||||||||||||||||||||||||||||||||||||||||||||||||||||||||||||||||||||||||||||||||||||||||||||||||||||||||||||||||||||||||||||||

Kestrel stirred in the new vibrations of her incarnation. She wasn't sure how long she'd been in this place without stars or planets. It was warm here and she could hear interesting rhythms and pulses. It was a new kind of music. And sometimes she heard other things. She did not enjoy some of those sounds. They were harsh and made the rhythms and pulses erratic.

Soon she sensed an awareness of Lucy, but it wasn't comfortable. Sound has changed so much, Kestrel thought, and everything seems tight somehow. She tried to move around in this watery home of hers. She could move. She was glad that hadn't changed. But instead of wanting to expand, and grow she wanted to become small. She wanted to disappear.

Uriel watched from above as Kestrel had been conceived and incarnated. Lucy and David were so wounded, so young and incredibly disconnected from each other and themselves. He waited for some hope that Kestrel would survive this experience.

This was the challenging part of being an angel. He could not interfere, even when he really wanted to. He could only watch and wait until he was asked for help. How he wished Kestrel had asked for his help before going to Earth once again. She'd been so focused on going that she'd asked for nothing beyond the details of her incarnation.

As Uriel watched, Lucy knelt by her bed. David had gone to work and Carrie was asleep. Lucy looked tired, and Uriel thought she should be sleeping too.

"Dear God," Lucy prayed, "I cannot see why you would have brought another child into our lives when things are so terrible. I don't know what I did to deserve this punishment. But, your will be done. If you want me to do this, please send me some help. I can't do this alone." Lucy placed her hands over her womb in an unconscious act of protection. The mother in her could not be denied – no matter how much fear clouded her life.

In answer to Lucy's prayer, Uriel placed his hands over hers. He hoped that Kestrel could feel his presence and be comforted as well. Now that help had been asked for he could offer his love and protection. He could at least bring help to Lucy. He hoped she had the ability to receive it.

Kestrel felt warmth move through her world and relaxed again. She sensed a familiar presence when this warmth flowed around her.

As Kestrel grew in the womb, she became more and more uncomfortable. She felt so restricted and the surges of energy that flowed around her often hurt.

She would try to make herself smaller to get away from the pain she couldn't see but could feel. It was very difficult here in this new world, so she would remind herself of floating through the Universe and how wonderful it was to feel so light and expansive. She remembered the joy. And when she felt its warmth move through her world, she remembered that she was loved by the Universe – and by Uriel.

And then the time came when she could not stay where she was anymore. She didn't know where she was going. There was a lot of pressure surrounding her and she sought whatever ease she could find. And then suddenly she felt cold. The familiar rhythms were replaced by an onslaught of harsh sounds and she couldn't feel the edges of her world anymore. She wanted to expand and see if she could once again float. But something hit her and then a terrible sound seemed to come from her. Air moved in and out of her. The light hurt her and strange sensations and voices surrounded her. Why am I here she wondered? She echoed her mother's familiar thought, "What did I do to deserve this?"

What did I do to deserve this? Yes, that was a song she already knew. She clung to it as she was cleaned, poked, prodded and finally wrapped in a blanket. Something strange was put in her mouth and she suckled. Her body began to feel more ease and she let herself drift. Uriel sent a song to comfort Kestrel as she drifted off to sleep. She couldn't remember exactly where she was going to, but it felt safe like home.

Lucy woke up from the anesthesia tired and depressed. Tomorrow she would have to go home and juggle two babies. Her feelings horrified her. She was a mother. She was supposed to feel love and joy and excitement. But she felt like crying. She reached for the rosary on her bedside table and began to pray. Comfort and ease surrounded her like soft wings and she fell into a restful sleep.

Over the next five years Lucy birthed four more children. Life wasn't easy with three boys and three girls all under the age of seven. But she had a purpose, a home and had learned to rely on her faith. The saints and angels had never let her down. Lucy convinced herself she had a very good life and had no right to ask for anything more. But there was always something brewing in the dark places of her heart that she refused to look at.

Kestrel, who they named Sharon, was what some called a frivolous child. She sang and danced. She often seemed to be in a world of her own. And there were times you could look in her eyes and see that she knew truths she shouldn't know. She had a wisdom that was easy to trust. It was uncanny to feel trust in a child that had done nothing in particular to earn it. She had so little experience. But her siblings, parents and many others leaned on that trust and began to rely on her. Some felt great comfort in this.

Others resented it and hardened their hearts towards her. Their fear made them wonder if she was evil.

Her parents saw her singing, dancing frivolity and they underestimated Sharon's practical nature. They punished her for not being serious enough. But they also expected her to shift the tensions in the family with her joyful presence. They did not understand Sharon's spirit. They worried that she would always have her head in the clouds and were afraid people would take advantage of her gifts – the one's they didn't understand but made use of when convenient.

One night, David woke Sharon from a sound sleep to spank her for forgetting to kiss Lucy goodnight. Lucy had cried about it instead of going up and kissing her daughter and tucking her in for the night. Sharon was five-years-old when she received this teaching about love's expectations and fear. She cried herself back to sleep and not just because she'd been spanked. Sharon knew in her heart that what he had done was not right. She felt deep in her bones that this was not her real home and she longed to return to the beauty of the home she remembered.

Kestrel was not the only one who cried that night. Uriel cried at her pain and regretted gifting her with remembering her true form before she came to Earth. If she did not remember the expansive joy and peace of her natural form, she would not feel the harsh difference in her current existence on Earth. Uriel's pain called like a beacon to the archangel, Raphael, who is a healer.

Raphael listened as Uriel spoke of his regret. Together they sent loving compassion to surround Kestrel's home and family in hopes that they would sense and absorb it. Then they sat in silence as each rebalanced their own heart.

And Raphael spoke:
"I believe Kestrel was right to request that she remember. Uriel, you see with great clarity the harsh difference between her life here and her life on Earth. However, I feel the healing power of her memories. They ease her heart and keep her spirit alive. Kestrel has great work to do in this incarnation.

"Her memories of this realm allow her to carry our vibrations. This energy signature gives her access to realms on Earth that will be very helpful to her as a Healer."

"What do you see?" Uriel asked with hope.

"I see that the Faery realm has taken notice of our Kestrel. They wait for an opportunity to teach her their healing ways. There will be at least three times in her life when she will have the opportunity to work with them. If she takes advantage of it, she will be well taken care of. Be at ease Uriel. It will be challenging for her. And, it will also have great rewards."

Over the years, as Uriel continued to watch over Kestrel, he saw the truth in Raphael's vision. When Kestrel was seven-years-old, she fell off a horse at a carnival and broke her clavicle. She had to lie flat on her back in a hospital for weeks until the bone was set. The Faeries came to her then and in her sleep took her to their realm and taught her much about healing. Kestrel had a natural gift and was quite powerful even at her young age. The Faeries blocked her memories of this time with them. They knew it would not be safe for her to talk of it at such a young age. The humans would teach her not to trust it.

And again, when Kestrel was eleven-years-old the Faeries came to teach her more. David took Sharon out of school for a week to plant the fields. The Faeries used their magic while she worked alone in the mornings and afternoons out in the fields planting. Anyone looking out would see Kestrel patiently planting row after row of peas and lettuce and beets. Kestrel would remember beginning each morning and afternoon. She would remember completing the rows after several hours work. But she would never quite remember the actual planting of all those seeds. For Kestrel was actually in the Faery world learning healing ways while the Faeries planted the seeds for her. Again they blocked her memories so that she had time to grow up and find her own life away from her family to do the work they knew she would love.

It was another 20 years before Kestrel found that she had a gift for healing. First, she needed to find her freedom.

Sharon was speaking to her father, David, about Mother's Day. He was angry. He said that she and the rest of her siblings were just a bunch of zeros. Sharon knew it wasn't true. She'd always known she had something special. But she could also feel herself contract away from his painful words. She felt herself shrink and diminish her life force. And in a moment of clarity she knew she must leave her family. If she did not, eventually she would believe that she was indeed a zero. And so she left.

Sharon began to try many new things. She started going out into the woods and to the beach by herself. She found peace and joy - her true nature. She talked to trees and clouds and seals and crows. The world opened to her in wondrous ways and she followed her heart without fear. She went to massage school and learned energetic healing, sound healing and the healing power of our thoughts. Kestrel discovered she had psychic and intuitive gifts.

As she continued her work, she noticed that she seemed to know things that she never remembered being taught. It made her uncomfortable to not know where her knowledge came from and so she resisted it. But when a client came to her with great need, she could not hold back. She followed her knowing even if she felt uneasy about it.

She so wanted to open to that knowing. But even though she was an alternative healer, she was also a scientist. She needed to know how she knew things she'd never been trained in. Without that knowing, she couldn't truly open to its power.

One day, she was talking about the time she fell off the horse and broke her clavicle to a friend, who was a gifted psychic. She told her friend that she always remembered that time with a sense of great joy. But it didn't make sense to her that a 5-year-old, who was used to having lots of brothers and sisters around, could lay still for weeks at a time and feel joyful about it. Her mother did not drive, so she was alone all day until her dad got off work, and they came to see her for a short time until visiting hours were over. For an active child, that time period should not have been a good memory.

Her friend got a far away look in her eyes and told Kestrel that she was not alone during that time. And although her body lay still in the bed, she was actually off in another place working with the Faeries.

As soon as she heard the words, Kestrel knew their truth and remembered joy bubbled and pulsed all through her. Yes. I learned it all there with them. I know why I know how to do things and where I learned them. It was a moment of tremendous freedom for Kestrel. She no longer needed to question her knowing. She didn't have a certificate on the wall proclaiming her competence. But she knew and that was enough.

Kestrel began to remember more than just her time with the Faeries. She also opened to memories of her other lives on Earth. She remembered simpler times when there was more ease and joy in life. She remembered what it felt like to live in loving community where every member was honored for the gifts they brought. She also remembered that she came from a star and that Earth was not really her home. Her earlier vague glimpses of other places and different ways of being became clear memories. For although Uriel did not block her memories of her true home, the trauma of birth had scattered them.

This time period was very painful for Kestrel. Her memories of past lives on Earth and her home with the stars made the fear and disconnection of those around her seem more terrible. Her desire to offer healing became fierce. And her hunger to know more about herself and her gifts led her back to her family.

It started with a dream. She stood in a cemetery at her ancestral home in northwest Ohio. Almost everyone in the cemetery was an ancestor, and they spoke to her. "There is something here for you, but it won't be here for long."

She called her father, David, and asked him where the family cemetery was. He asked her, "Which one? There are five." Before she realized it, Sharon asked David if he wanted to go on a road trip and visit

them. She knew she had to go, and she needed a
guide. And so they went. And David did his best to
give Sharon space and let her do whatever it was she
did. He didn't understand it, but he was glad to have
this chance to do the trip with her.

As David took her to the five cemeteries and spoke
about his ancestors, Sharon discovered that there
were other healers in the family: an aunt and uncle
who were chiropractors, a grandmother who was
known for her special healing soup and a grandfather
who could grow anything.

And when she stayed with her mother's sister, Sharon
learned about the cousin who did Tarot readings in
Toledo and heard lots of stories about psychic
happenings among many different family members.
Sharon discovered that her gifts were inherited from
both sides of her family. It made her feel more
connected to her family and less like the odd duck.
Her elderly aunt was the only one who openly spoke
about this heritage. She died the following winter.

For the next seven years Sharon, who now felt a
stronger claim to her gifts, worked diligently to
develop them. She became a powerful healer and
teacher. She traveled to sacred sites and learned from
the land. While in England at Stonehenge, she even
learned that her name was once Kestrel.

Sharon offered her healing abilities to her family
when they were ill. Some accepted her offer and were

amazed at her abilities. But they didn't really understand what she did or where her gifts came from. This made them afraid.

Sharon felt their fear so made herself smaller to ease them. It seemed like such a little thing to not talk about what she did and who she truly was when at family gatherings. But over time and without realizing it she gave up other little pieces of herself. If she shared news of her accomplishments, they ignored her or changed the subject. They slowly started giving her presents that were an insult to who she was and what she believed and practiced. She knew it was fear or ignorance that motivated them. She understood historically where that fear came from, so she let it go. Sharon knew they wanted her to be like them, so they gave her gifts they would like, and they only spoke to her of things they understood in her life.

And Sharon became a smaller and smaller version of herself. She was not able to hold the power of her work in the same way, and she became afraid. She doubted her abilities. She kept herself from doing things that would make her visible. Soon her clients and students could not even find her. And Sharon's fear grew. She feared mostly that she was failing, that she had lost her path and purpose, and her work in the world would never be complete. Sharon's fear fed on the fears of her family, and the family welcomed that fear for it made Sharon seem more a part of them.

Sharon became ill, and the family took care of some of her physical needs for a short while. Her illness made it difficult to move. She felt so heavy and so small. She slept a lot. And in her dreams she went home and 127sometimes she remembered what it was like to be expansive and dance with the stars.

Uriel and Raphael became quite concerned about Kestrel. She seemed to be disappearing in Sharon's life. They knew if she didn't connect to her true nature and do it soon that her light could go out forever. But they had to allow Kestrel her free will. They sent her love but could do nothing else without interfering.

The Faeries were also aware of Kestrel's danger and they didn't have to abide by the same rules as the angels did. They tried to tempt her by infusing more beauty in the natural world around her. Kestrel noticed the beauty but was not quite able to engage with it or to take it in for any length of time. The Faeries entered her dreams and reminded her of the times they had spent together. Kestrel would wake up feeling a sense of joy, but the fear would soon dampen the joy.

One morning however, Sharon awoke to crows cawing and reached out to them as friends. It made her smile, and she wondered when she had stopped talking to the crows. It made her sad to notice she'd stopped. And fear rose in a particular way that made her feel trapped. She could feel it like a strong band of rubber all around her. It was terrible, and it made her tired. She was lost and needed help. Sharon felt hopeless and asked spirit to help her.

Uriel danced for joy! She did it. She asked for help. And Uriel helped her in two ways. He kept sending her dreams of when she was a light being at home dancing and singing with the stars. And he also nudged her into situations with her family so that she could see their fear for what it was. This went on for weeks until Sharon's baby sister, who she loved dearly, spoke about feeling alone in a corner unnoticed when she was a child. Her sister's story broke her heart. She felt it break into pieces. It had to break, so Sharon could let out all the love she felt for her sister. That love was a light and it made a beautiful sound. It reminded Sharon that she was Kestrel. It reminded her that she could choose joy. She could choose to radiate and share joy.

Sharon began to feel into it and started to expand until she hit that band of rubber, which seemed impenetrable. She could smell and taste the fear. It was so powerful. It seemed easier to back off and get smaller again. She retreated and looked around at her gathered family. They had spent the afternoon together, and everyone was in pain and discomfort. No one really felt safe to share anything real about his or her lives. Even her baby sister's comment was said in a joking manner, so no one would really notice. But Sharon noticed and could not live with her sister feeling like she didn't matter.

Anger took hold and Sharon used it to burn through the rubbery band of fear that blocked her from her own true nature. She expanded and let her light and love shine. She knew this meant leaving her family once again but Sharon couldn't turn back. They were all welcome to follow her out of fear, but she knew most of them wouldn't.

Part of Kestrel wanted to go home now that she had learned how fear could become so overpowering. Sharon went to bed that night and fell asleep in complete exhaustion. After a couple hours, she began to dream. Uriel entered that dream.

"You can come home now, if you choose," he said.

"I want to come," Kestrel said. "But I'm not sure that it's time."

"Have you learned what you came to learn?" he asked.

"I think I have. I understand that joy is something to wield – not as a weapon against fear, but as a tool to balancing it. Fear, you see, is a contraction. It is meant to stop us and make us look around for danger. Fear is a valuable tool in itself. It is not meant to stay around but rather to invite us to take time for caution and evaluation. If we listen to fear and hear its message, it will move on and we can expand once again into our purpose.

"Most people hold on to fear. It gets stuck and builds up and in seeing the danger in that, fear cries out again. When we ignore its cries, we are abusing fear and diminishing its purpose. We need to face our fear, listen to its message and then move on into what gives us joy and purpose.

Photo by Lisa Langel

"I was very stuck in fear. I think I tried to carry my family's fears. I know I stopped being myself because it raised their already overwhelming fear."
Kestrel sat quietly in her own thoughts. Uriel felt her sorrow and sang softly to ease her pain. She cried great tears and released some of that sorrow.

"It is so heavy," she sobbed. "Built up fear weighs everything down. I remember feeling that in my mother's womb. And when the fear would spike the sounds around me would feel like shattered glass falling. I tried to make myself very small to get away.

Then something would remind me of home and of you, and I'd find my joy again."

"I sent love and healing energy to your mother," Uriel explained. "She asked for help when she first learned she was pregnant with you. So I sent it to her with the hope that you would also feel it. You forgot to ask for help too often. Next time, my dear, remember to ask for my help before you incarnate. It will ease my heart."

Kestrel gave him a watery smile and leaned into him.

"Moving into our joy is a courageous thing to do sometimes," she whispered. "But it feels so good to expand and to dance in one's fullness!"

Kestrel twirled and expanded her light with great joy. She felt like a cat in morning's first stretch. Sitting again next to Uriel, she sighed with satisfaction. "I won't come home yet," she decided. "I have learned what I wanted to learn, but I do not have enough experience with the lesson to feel that I truly know it. And, although I used my gifts very well for a time and helped a lot of people, I can do a lot more to transform fear on Earth."
Uriel nodded in acknowledgment of her decision.

"But before you leave me, and I wake up again," she laughed, "I'm asking for your help, and Raphael's help, and the Faeries' help. I know what I'm in for, and how easy it can be to absorb the pain around me and to get mired down in its heavy fear vibrations. I willingly ask for and accept the help of all my guides and allies."

Kestrel tilted her head and looked deeply into Uriel's eyes.

"How's your heart?" she asked.

"Much better now," he smiled. He held her eyes and radiated his deep love for her as he slowly faded from her dream.

Sharon woke up in her bed and stretched like a cat after a good night's sleep. Her heart still felt heavy at the knowledge she must leave her family and the fear in which they surrounded themselves. But her grief had shifted. Beneath it she felt the strong pulse of hope and joy. She greeted the crows outside her window, breathed in the beauty of the trees and stepped once more into the power of her gifts and knowing.

Raphael moved to Uriel's side, and together they watched Kestrel claim her true nature once again in this incarnation.

"You were right," Uriel admitted. "She is able to meet her challenges and she has found great gifts."

"You weren't wrong," Raphael said. "She does keenly feel the harsh difference between the rampant fear on the dark planet and the expansive joy of her existence here. It brings her pain. It also inspires her to facilitate change. She's quite remarkable really."

## Joy is a Wellspring

Here in love's body,
in the silence of deep listening,
in the space between inhale and exhale,
joy is a wellspring.

Joy bubbles up in unexpected rhythms
bursting from my heart –
sometimes like a geyser: untamable, undeniable.

Sometimes joy is the softest trickle
bringing such sweet delight that life will never be
the same.

Here in love's field, I drink in joy
sending my taproots to gather
every drop of juicy, sweet nurture.

I carry this wellspring within me.
I am a bringer of joy, radiating it wherever I go
without fear or caution or hesitation.
I am a bringer of joy. So be it.

~ Kestrel

# About the Author

C. Rhalena Renee (Lena) was raised in Ohio and has lived most of her adult life in the Pacific Northwest. She finds her joy in  traveling, singing, writing, and teaching. She feels most fully alive when co-creating playful, quiet, wild and/or reflective work to encourage every person in owning their unique significance and purpose.

Knowing that we learn best when we engage the senses and move from the heart, Lena uses storytelling, music and ritual to invite participants into the dance of being fully alive.

Photo by Elizabeth Dobes

Lena grew up farming, hiking and camping. She is connected deeply to the land and knows the bounty of lessons one can learn from Nature. As an anthropologist she studied with many indigenous traditions, which deepened her understanding of the web of life. Finding our place on that web is a wonderful step into deep joy.

As spiritual healer, teacher and anthropologist, Lena brings multicultural experiences to open the mind and heart through poetry, movement and story.

*Choices for Joy* is the first of 3 books in the Vibrant Living Series. *Emotional Landscapes*, book 2, will invite the reader into an adventure where one uses all their emotions as reliable allies in navigating life and its choices. *The Call to Create* is the third and final book in the series. It focuses on the importance of offering ourselves in service to our community in ways that richly and ecstatically serve us.

Find C. Rhalena Renee at WhispersOfTheSoul.us

Contact her for speaking engagements, workshops, playshops, creative encounters or book signing events.

56287442R00083

Made in the USA
Charleston, SC
18 May 2016